Not A Blog... Not an Article...

...It's a Blarticle®

45 Quick, Powerful Lessons in Persuasion, Performance, & Personal Growth

from Best-Selling Author
Rob Jolles

Copyright © 2025 by Rob Jolles

All rights reserved.

No part of this book may be reproduced in any form or by any electronic or mechanical means, including information storage and retrieval systems, without written permission from the author, except for the use of brief quotations in a book review.

Published in the United States by Pinnacle Insights Publishing

ISBN 979-8-9929257-0-8

Contents

Dedication	vii
Acknowledgments	ix
Preface	xi

Persuasion

Proud to Sell: Reclaiming the Honor in Selling	3
Don't Want To Be Sold? Be Careful What You Wish For	7
A Rate Book And A Yellow Pad Of Paper	11
It's Time To Pitch The Word "Pitch"	15
Can Anybody Sell?	19
The Two Ways To Motivate Others	23
Want To Measure Your Sales Aptitude? Try Using A Chess Clock	27
Everybody Has A Story…	31
Asking Almost The Right Question	33
Is It A Conversation Or An Interrogation?	37
The Line In The Sand	41
A Most Unusual Nickname	45
Asking Disturbing Questions - Is It Mean, Or Is It Merciful?	49
When More Is Not Better	51
Don't Sell Me Things	55

Performance

The Perfect Performance Combination	61
The Effort Behind Effortless	65
Running Your Race	67
Looking To Nail Your Next Presentation? Lock It Down	71
A Two-Word Response To Pressure	75
The Most Important Question Rarely Asked	79
The Three Levels Of Greed	83
Honesty Is Not Always The Best Policy	87
The Art Of Making Your Message Stick	91

You Can't Hug A Porcupine	93
The Great Equalizers	95
Let Them See You Sweat!	97
It's All In The Timing	99
Not Leaving Well Enough Alone	103
A Reason To Try	105

Personal Growth

Is There A Penalty For Hope?	109
A Tale of Two Stories	111
Taming The Victim Voice	115
What Would You Attempt To Do…	119
You Snooze, You Lose	121
Going To Your Off-Hand	123
The Schmuck Running In The Rain	127
The Pig Farmer And The Intellectual	131
The Cost Of Being Right	135
The Pursuit Of Imperfection	139
The Communication Shot Clock	143
Playing The Course – Not The Opponent	147
The Fisherman's Bucket	151
Getting Good At Doing Things Badly	153
The Perfect Underdog	157
Final Thoughts	161
Also by Rob Jolles	163
About Jolles Associates, Inc.	165

Praise for It's a Blarticle®!

"This book is a treasure trove of practical wisdom and powerful insights from Rob, delivered in a way that's easy to absorb and apply. Each idea stands on its own, yet together they form a dynamic blueprint for mastering communication and excelling in sales. Whether you're a seasoned professional or just starting out, this book will elevate your skills and set you apart."

— Greg Heffington, Founder, Heffington Consulting

"I am a big fan of Rob Jolles' Blarticles®, as I am of almost everything he has published. His messages are crisp, to the point, and valuable for sales professionals, business owners and anyone else who is looking to improve their revenue generation performance."

— Fred Diamond Institute for Effective Professional Selling.

"Finally! A compendium of the best of Rob Jolles' Blarticles. His authentic writing consistently teaches something new, encourages introspection, and always inspires. Once you pick this up, you'll want to binge the whole book."

— Dana Klein CEO and Founder, Klein Strategies

"I'm a raving fan of Rob Jolles' Blarticles® because they're authentic, sincere, and thought-provoking. In a world flooded with content, his Blarticles® always stand out. I look forward to them, knowing I'll learn something valuable—and I often share them with colleagues. Always insightful; always worth the read!"

— Neil B. Wood Founder Neil Wood Consulting Amazon Best-selling author of *Best Practices of Successful Financial Advisors*

"Rob has a knack for delivering insightful, relevant, and truly valuable information in a way that just sticks with you. His Blarticles® are pure genius—they grab your attention instantly and pack expert advice into bite-sized, impactful takeaways. What really sets Rob apart, though, is how he challenges you to step into the client's shoes, shifting your perspective for more meaningful and productive interactions."

— Phyllis Mikolaitis Vice President Marketing Development Pinnacle Solutions/ Sustaining Peak Performance

Dedication

NO WRITER WRITES ALONE...

This book is dedicated to those who have followed my journey, read my Blarticles®, challenged my ideas, and shared their own. You have taught me invaluable lessons, allowed me to teach in return, and inspired me with your stories. You have graciously let me write about you, shaping these pages with their experiences. This collection is for you. Your engagement, insights, and support have made every word worth writing.

Acknowledgments

I would like to acknowledge the following:

- First, and foremost, my wife Ronni. For close to two decades, she has quietly, and confidently edited every single Blarticle® written, skillfully maneuvering around my fragile writer's ego, and providing the editing assistance I so badly needed.

- Blarticles® are derived from interactions, and these interactions are with friends, colleagues, clients, audience members and more. You may not have known it, but I really was listening… and taking notes. Thank you all for all those conversations!

- Finally, to my prep and publishing assistant, Mary Miller. As someone who thought he knew a lot about the publishing world, I was humbled by how much I had yet to learn about this particular process. From formatting to cover design to submission—and the countless questions I had along the way—Mary was there with a patient ear and a confident answer. Her guidance made all the difference.

Preface

Ready for this? I don't like blogs. I've never liked blogs. For years, I had various editors, publicists, business consultants, and family members pushing me to write blogs… and I steadfastly refused! What's my problem with blogs? That's simple. In the blogs I was reading, there were interesting stories, but nothing in it for the reader.

I come from a world of W.I.F.M.'s. That's an acronym that stands for this: What's in it for me!" This is an acronym that is well known to those in sales, and to professional speakers. Traveling between both of those worlds, I've become a subject matter expert on the subject of W.I.F.M's.

For instance, when you meet with a client who doesn't know you, you've got about 30-seconds to answer the question, "What's in it for me?" Otherwise, the meeting is over before it even starts. When you're delivering a presentation, you've got about two-minutes to get at that W.I.F.M. If you don't, those who don't *walk* out will *check* out, and those who don't check out, will *act* out.

From the moment I was introduced to blogs, my dislike for them centered around the fact that far too often, there were no W.I.F.M.'s to be found – anywhere. I found that there was no real message, lots of poor grammar, a lot of self-promotion, no compelling hook, inconsistent posting, and worst of all, they lacked a conversational tone. Instead, I was reading about bloggers writing about tuna sandwiches they liked. I actually like tuna sandwiches, but I was discouraged by

Preface

the whole concept of blogging. Truth be told, I don't even like the word, "blog."

You may be wondering, "Aren't I about to read a book of blogs from this guy who apparently has an aversion to blogs?" Please understand there are a few things I *do* like about blogs. For one, I happen to like the delivery mechanism a blog provides. Unlike random articles that appear anywhere, those who actually take their blogs seriously tend to post what they write on a regular basis, and in a regular location. Score one for blogs!

I also believe that, much like athletes that need to train to stay sharp, writers need to write to stay sharp. I have a handful of books I've written over the years, but to be clear, I'm not always writing books. Writing smaller pieces like these keeps me in what I call, "writing shape." Another point for blogs.

Finally, I believe writing blogs can make you a bit wiser. I do not claim to be a genius, but writing blogs has made me, "methodically observant." I take lots of notes, and the idea behind taking these notes is to try and learn from them. You see, that's how I think people become wiser. It doesn't come from making mistakes or not making mistakes. It comes from being consciously aware of the successes you are enjoying, the failures you are enduring, and most importantly, the lessons learned from each. That actually tracks my definition of wisdom. Blogs score again.

With blogs scoring enough points to at least give it a try, I decided to do just that… with some rules:

1. My first rule was to try and honor the personal nature of a blog. That meant, I wanted to make sure each piece brought in personal stories, favorite quotes, interesting analogies, to name a few.

2. My second, and most important rule, was to provide value. I tried to use the stories I was sharing to simplify complicated

subjects. I wanted to inform, and stimulate, reflection. I wanted every blog to address the question, "What's in it for me to read this?" I wanted to make absolutely sure to deliver on that question.

3. My third and final rule was to keep my blogs short. I had written plenty of articles with word-counts in the thousands. I decided to try and keep every piece I wrote under 750 words… usually.

So, on August 5th, 2010, I took the plunge. Every story begins somewhere, and for me, this was the first blog I ever wrote. It was so long ago; within the story you can sense I was still trying to figure out what I was doing. One thing was clear; I was searching for a message…

The Real Story

I promised I would not write this particular piece. I promised my niece Stacy, and I promised myself. Who needs to hear about some pathetic mishap on another road trip? Nope, I wasn't going to write about this one… that is until I figured out what the real message of this particular near catastrophe was. The sad part of the story goes like this:

Rob finishes his seminar in New York. Rob meets up with family. Rob and family take the Long Island Railroad to Long Beach to spend a few days with their friends. Rob helps family with their luggage and finds his laptop bag with the most important items he possesses is no longer on the train. In 25 years of travel Rob has never had a lost bag, let alone one that has kept in his possession. Rob is devastated, but that's not the story here.

The happy part of the story goes like this. Thirty minutes later, while being consoled by his friend, and waiting for the police to file a report, Rob's phone rings. It turns out someone saw the laptop bag away from the other bags, and after asking the person closest to it if it was his, (who was not Rob), decides to, "protect it," removes it from the train, and takes it home. Twenty minutes later Rob and his laptop bag with the most important items he possesses are back in his hands again. Oh, and Rob isn't just happy; Rob is beside himself with jubilation. As a matter of fact, Rob is happier than he has been for quite some time. Yes, Rob is elated, but that's not the story here either.

Wasn't having finished a successful seminar good enough? No industry has been hit harder than the seminar and travel industry, and yet here I was finishing my best month of consulting in a year and a half without any real celebration or fanfare.

Wasn't meeting up with my wife and daughter for a nice trip with wonderful friends good enough? Spending time away with your loved ones usually puts a smile on most people's faces including mine, and yet I was almost going through the motions of affection to both.

Wasn't going to see two of our closest friends on the face of the earth in their beautiful waterfront home good enough? These are friends we have seen at least a couple times a year for over 25 years, and always have a wonderful time when we are together, and yet I was focused on the long train ride to see them. It was a 45-minute train ride.

All these wonderful blessings and yet having my laptop bag missing for about thirty minutes – and then finding it is what it took to make me truly happy. And that's the story.

Why is it that we practically sleepwalk our way through things that

Preface

we should rejoice in and are not truly happy until something is taken away... and given back to us? How often do we take stock in our good health after a health scare? How often do we thank our lucky stars for the job we have after our name does not appear on a list of layoffs?

I'm happy to have been reunited with my laptop bag, computer, air mouse, keys, cords, books, sunglasses, credit cards, and more. However, I'm even happier that I not only figured out what the real story was, I'm going to keep that message front and center.

With a personal story, with a defined message, and under 750 words... usually, there was one, last obstacle to get over before I ever called myself a *blogger*, and that was to under no circumstances call myself a *blogger*. I never liked that word, and still don't. I knew I was utilizing some aspects of a blog, and some aspects of an article, so I decided to invent my own word for what I was trying to do, and trademark it. And so, after a little bit of legal assistance, I became the proud father of the word Blarticle®; pronounced blahr-ti-k*uh*-l.

Decades later, it not only has a place in our vernacular, it's kind of catchy when you think about it. Say it five times and you'll see what I mean. Webster's Dictionary doesn't recognize it as a word... yet, but the Urban Dictionary does!

For the record, I didn't trademark the word Blarticle® to keep people from using it. I just didn't want to spend decades creating this version of writing, only to have another company trademark the word and force *me* to stop using it. I invite you to use the word Blarticle®. Just put a "®" after the word.

So, there you have it. The first Blarticle® ever written, and the story behind the Blarticle®. The story behind this book is a simpler one. After decades of faithfully writing Blarticles®, I decided to cherry-pick some of my favorites, and offer them to you. Because I tend to

Preface

write in three different arenas, you'll see Blarticles® in three different sections:

- Persuasion. I learned to love selling from the New York Life Insurance company, learned how to sell from Xerox, and learned to appreciate selling from my dad, Lee Jolles. Here you will find fifteen separate Blarticles® centering on persuasion, influence, and selling.
- Performance. After completing my sale career, I spent close to a decade as a sales trainer for Xerox, and learned from some of the greatest trainers I'd ever meet how to conduct myself as a professional. I went on to spend over three decades as a professional speaker, traveling over three million miles in the air conducting keynotes, and workshops all over the world. Here you will find fifteen separate Blarticles® centering on mastering the art of motivating, inspiring, and teaching others.
- Personal Growth. Do something long enough, and live the life of an entrepreneur, and you'll pick up a tip or two about overcoming obstacles, embracing change, and developing resilience to mention a few. Here you will find fifteen separate Blarticles® centering on complex personal growth principles, and applying practical strategies to become more effective in both your personal and professional life.

Enjoy your journey; I hope you enjoy reading them as much I did writing them, and in true Blarticle® fashion, I hope you learn a few things while you're at it!

Preface

```
Blarticle® - noun
: a hybrid between a blog and an article - a concise,
impactful piece of writing that delivers meaningful
insights in a way that is both engaging and
educational - in 750 words or less.
```

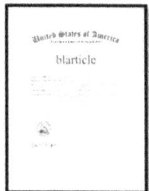

There are close to 450 Blarticles® in this world now, and if you'd like to get on the mailing list to receive notice each time a new one appears, just go to the site, and sign up!

https://jolles.com/blarticle/

Persuasion

This section of the book explores the true essence of selling—moving beyond outdated tactics and reclaiming the honor within the profession. It challenges common misconceptions, delves into the psychology of motivation, and reinforces that great salespeople don't just sell—they solve, serve, and inspire.

Why are so many salespeople afraid of being called salespeople? My father was a salesman—an incredible one—and he made me proud to embrace the title. If you've ever doubted the value of this profession, this one's for you when you read...

Proud to Sell: Reclaiming the Honor in Selling

I had the pleasure of working with two salespeople this week I respect immensely. At one point our conversation seemed to move towards why salespeople are so nervous about being called salespeople. My father was an amazing salesman and made me proud to be called a salesman.

The fact is, there are good lawyers, and bad lawyers, but we need people from time to time to help us interpret the law. There are good police, and bad police, but we need people to help enforce the law. There are good salespeople, and bad salespeople, but we need people who can ask us questions we aren't asking ourselves, problem solve, and move us past our fear of change.

What follows is something I wrote a few years ago after I had to listen to someone who was berating the industry I care so much about. If you have ever had a crisis of confidence, or question for an instant why the profession of selling, and I mean selling the right way is vital to so many, this one is for you.

"Who Am I?"

I prevent financial tragedies every time I find a way to get you to finally believe that your retirement and children's education are more important than a seven-day cruise.

I save lives every time I persuade someone to stop putting off "what if" and purchase an item that protects themselves and their loved ones.

I assist companies each time I am able to get a decision maker to look at the "big picture" and make decisions that reflect total costs to the customer.

I looked you in the eye and asked you some disturbing questions. It upset you, but your anger towards me saved your life and the life of others on a road you would have been too drunk to drive on.

I'm the person in the store. You felt put off by all my questions but wound up with a solution that not only saved your business that day, but saved your job a year later as my product expanded along with your business.

I'm the person who changed your mind about skimping on a document that later was responsible for bringing you your biggest customer.

I'm the kid standing in the rain outside your door at home. By creating a commitment based on shear pity, I took some of your money that later saved a tiny piece of land in a small natural paradise.

Not a Blog ~ Not an Article ~ A Blarticle®

I put up with the stereotypical fallacies that have portrayed me as a buffoon when, in actuality, I was the only one who provided for the future of your family when an early death might have meant devastating and dramatic changes in your loved one's worlds.

I could have taken no for an answer and sometimes I wish I had. I could not because I had seen the personal tragedy of procrastination.

I have empathy for your fear of change because I have similar fears. The fear of the unknown sometimes outweighs the pain of the present. It is my job to move you past these fears and get you to take action in an ethical manner.

I may not be apparent to all, but I exist in everyone's soul.

Who am I?
I am a salesperson.

I get it; there are still a lot of people who still don't understand how important a well-trained salesperson can be in his or her decision-making process. But when one of the biggest banks in the nation doesn't understand it, well, that just doesn't sit well with me. Want to hear what an annoyed Rob Jolles sounds like? You will when you read…

Don't Want to be Sold? Be Careful What You Wish For

There I was sitting down with a nice cup of coffee and watching a ballgame when an advertisement came on the air from not just any bank, but my bank. It turns out Capital One bank is really going to shake up the banking industry.

According to Capital One, "all banks feel the same" and that's why "Capital One is building something completely different; Capital One cafes." Sounds good so far! The commercial continues to give you a visual look of what they call, "banking reimagined," and they aren't kidding! The lobby looks more like a WeWork facility, with couches, bar tables, snacks, juices, coffee, and more. What an amazing way to reimagine banking… and then it all goes wrong with one, irresponsible statement:

"Ready to help you; not sell you."

Really? You want to *help us*, but not *sell us*? Pardon me, but that sure sounds like an oxymoron. How can you help us if you are unwilling to sell us? Could it be you are as misinformed as to what good sales people do as some of the customers you have a responsibility to help? Interestingly enough, it's those exact people who need your help the most.

I get the fact that some of the public is misinformed and believes that being sold something is some sort of evil and devious act. But you – one of the largest banks in the country – *you* don't understand how misguided a statement like that is?

- It's a trained salesperson who isn't afraid to ask you tougher questions that aren't always pleasant but are questions you are not prepared to ask yourself.
- It's a trained salesperson who understands your fear of change, and has the skillset to persuade, and the courage to utilize these skills in the best interest of the customer.
- It's a trained salesperson who understands that you need to go further than looking at "what is," and instead help to you address "what if?"
- It's a trained salesperson who helps you make decisions that are proactive, not reactive.
- It's a trained salesperson who doesn't take "no" for an answer, and asks more questions to help better understand the real reason for that "no."

Where are my manners? Perhaps Capital One is right, and people who are "ready to help you; not sell you" would better serve you and act on the instructions you provide them. For the record, that's the definition of an order-taker, so make sure you study up, so you can tell your order taker how to handle your finances. After all, we're only talking about your hard-earned money, your home, your car, your children's education, your retirement, and more. But hey, I hear they may even be serving smoothies. I love smoothies!

As for me, I not only value to assistance of salespeople, I'll gladly pay extra for their assistance. I welcome their assistance because I don't want an order taker handling my banking. Ask your tougher questions, and push me when I need to be pushed because ultimately, I believe it's one of the sincerest acts of kindness you can offer another human being.

Capital One, I love the idea of a café, and I'm not afraid of "reimagining banking" but I truly hope you reconsider your reckless views regarding selling, and amend your catchy little slogan. I'd suggest this one:

"Ready to help you; and not afraid to persuade you."

W e all know that changes in life are inevitable. But change is not always perfect, and sometimes there are important things lost when we make a change. I'd like to tell you about something we did lose as a result of change, and lessons we can all learn from it when you read...

A Rate Book and a Yellow Pad of Paper

"If you can't explain it simply, you don't understand it well enough."

— ALBERT EINSTEIN

I was twenty-two years old when I graduated from the University of Maryland. Within two weeks, I found myself working as a salesman for the New York Life Insurance Company. I was quickly given a spot in a bullpen with a dozen other salespeople, and I was given a desk, a phone, and a phonebook. If you're wondering where the computer was,  I must tell you that no salesman or office had a computer at that time. I repeat; not one computer to be found. Within two years, this was all about to change, but I consider myself fortunate to have sold at this time, and I'll tell you why.

When salespeople in our office prepared to meet with their clients, they did so in a far different way than you might imagine. A typical preparation consisted of packing a rate book to figure out a client's premium, an application to write the policy on, and a nice clean yellow pad of paper.

If, by chance, a client wanted an illustration of future dividend projections or cash values (known as a policy illustration,) you went to the general office for their assistance. You provided the administrative people with ages and names, the information was phoned to New York, and you waited. You could get a verbal answer or two on the phone, but a typical policy illustration took about a week to return in the mail.

Unencumbered with stacks of data, customers talked of problems and needs while salespeople talked of concepts and solutions. In those next few moments, something occurred that has since become rare. People sold - and they sold based on who they were, not how computer literate they were.

It was tragic to me to see so many of our most talented and tenured salespeople become casualties during the computer revolution of the early eighties. Many from this generation of sales veterans had ten times the product knowledge of their competition. They had experience and business savvy that was light-years ahead of those they were competing with. What they did *not* have were pages and pages of illustrations with projected dividend options, and multiple cash values based on projected interest rates. They could not quickly manipulate an interest rate or payment amount. Then again, most of them would not have, even if they had the knowledge. It just was not how they conducted business. They were the true heroes of the selling profession, and when the computers came in, a generation of tremendous sales professionals was lost. They became obsolete overnight, and unwilling to change their ways, quietly faded away. My father, Lee Jolles, was one of them.

I am all for technology, and I was one of those "young whippersnappers" who embraced this change, and fought his battles with his new computer. In retrospect, it diminished my selling abilities, and contributed to making me more of a computing machine that made more eye contact with his screen than his client, rather than a trusted business advisor. Remember, machines have no feelings. I lost who I was and I lost the empathy I once displayed with my customers as well. I even lost my yellow pad of paper.

When it comes to change, I don't want to sound like the old man standing in front of his house shouting, "Get off my lawn!" Change is often inevitable, and ultimately, we adjust our ways to allow technology to enhance what we do. Used properly, this technology should mean better service and improved efficiency. Those who are careful to blend technology with old school attention continue to display honor within selling.

And so, standing on my lawn, watching you walk by, with one eyebrow up in the air, I leave you with this one last reminder: The next meeting you have with a client, there will be a time to Google and gather the data you feel is necessary. But before you break out your laptop, tablet, or other display of data to show the client how smart you are, take out something else first. Take out your yellow pad of paper and listen without the distraction of the computer screen: Your reward will be the connection you make with the client and the trust you will be building by having a true conversation.

Sometimes life can be a real "pitch", but if you are actually still using that word, and abiding by its actions, you're going to get an earful when you read…

It's Time to Pitch the Word "Pitch"

I received an email from a good friend who asked me a question I'd like to share with you. She asked me what I thought of the word, "pitch." She was relating it to a salesperson she worked with who had an uncanny way of not just using this word to describe his daily sales activities, but revel in it as well. He just LOVES getting in to see a client,  and pitching away! Not being one to shy away from an opportunity to provide an opinion, I presented my opinion in three words. "I hate it." I can hear my mother right now saying, "Hate is such a strong word. Can't you come up some others instead?" So, to respect my mother, I'll give it a try. How about four words, "I'm offended by it."

Let's do a little test. What is the first thing that comes to your mind when you hear the word, "pitch?" Something tells me those first words were not, "ask questions" or "listen." Maybe I'm too emotional here, so let's consult Webster's Dictionary and make sure we're defining the word correctly. Webster's defines "pitch" this way: "a high-pressure sales talk."

Imagine setting up a meeting with a client and telling them, "For the record, I intend to have a high-pressure sales talk with you!" Sounds like a surefire approach to not getting past the first phone call to me. I suppose you could just surprise them with your "pitch", but I think you get the point here. If this is something we have no intention of doing, and it's offensive to anyone you do speak with, why is the word still even around?

I suppose the word "pitch" has its place on QVC or a good infomercial. The late Billy Mays was one of the best pitchmen who ever lived. I never got the sense that sitting with Billy would provide a whole lot of banter back and forth, nor did I see him as a champion consultant, but man that guy could pitch! In fact, he was the perfect pitchman. He could out talk, out shout, and out last anyone who stepped up to his booth. I wouldn't recommend any sound minded sales person to step into a client's office and shout, "HI, ROB JOLLES HERE FOR ANYBODY'S FUNDS, AND DO I HAVE PRODUCT FOR YOU!!!"

The irony here is that true selling in its purest form could not be further from the concept of a "pitch." In fact, it's the complete opposite. Instead of talking, it involves listening. Instead of pushing a one idea fits all scheme, it involves shaping the solution to fit the client's specific needs. Instead of obsession on a solution, it involves studying a client's potential problems.

Want to know why sales people get a bad name? It's because clients are afraid they are going to have to talk on the phone, or sit face-to-face with some knucklehead who wants to "pitch" something to them.

When I conduct two-day workshops that teach people to sell, I teach opening tactics, closing tactics, objection-handling tactics, ways to create trust, ways to create urgency, and more. Over those sixteen hours guess how much time I spend on the actual solution, or for the sake of this Blarticle® the "pitch?" About ten minutes, and I feel as if I'm probably giving it too much time at that. When you have worked hard and done all the real work that skilled sales people use to earn the right to discuss a solution with another person, shouldn't the solution be the easiest part of the conversation?

I suppose well before my time when Fuller Brush, vacuum, bible, and a litany of other door-to-door sales people roamed the earth, getting a foot in the door, and wowing someone with a well-rehearsed "pitch" probably showed some promise. But, along with the yellow leisure suits that accompanied these sales, we've moved on. So, I'll finish this week's Blarticle® with a "pitch" of my own…

Step right up, make a commitment, and join the millions who have said, "no" to the word, "pitch!" Eliminate that word from your vocabulary and you'll not only spare yourself the embarrassment of informing your clients you have little to no interest in their needs, you'll demonstrate a true understanding of what your real role with that client is in the first place. Do it today, and I'll even throw in a spiral slicer… but you must act now!

Remember this slogan… "If life's a pitch, then you die."

When you spend your career working with salespeople, some of the questions you hear can sound a bit repetitive. However, there is one question that I hear more than any other. The answer is absolutely critical to your success, whether you sell or not. I'll not only tell you what the question is, but I'll also provide a simple answer when you read…

Can Anybody Sell?

After over 30 years of teaching professional sales training, I'd like to answer the most often asked question. This question can be asked in various ways, such as, "Are you born a good salesperson?" or "Is the art of selling a natural skill?" Any way you slice it; the question really remains the same: "Can anybody sell?" If I had a nickel for every time  I was asked that question, well, let's just say that I'd have a heck of a lot of nickels!

I'm not sure I knew the answer myself, until I was fortunate enough to meet someone whom I consider to be the greatest salesman who ever lived. No, it wasn't any of the published authors and professional speakers whose fraternity I too belong. Nope, it was a fellow named Ben Feldman.

You probably haven't heard of him, but you should have. In 1979, while I was with the New York Life Insurance Company, Ben led the industry in sales – and that included the sales of *all* insurance companies. Actually, it is unfair to say he led the industry; he dominated it. Ben Feldman tripled the next closest competitor, and according to the Bureau of Labor Statistics, that was well over 250,000 agents.

I had never seen a picture of Ben, but I imagined what he looked like; outgoing, tall, aggressive, big booming voice… like me! (Okay, maybe not me, but I do have a booming voice.) I guess I imagined he would be a collection of every stereotype I had been led to believe was necessary to be an effective salesperson. One day, I had the rare pleasure of meeting this man, and in a way, he changed my life. Ben Feldman stood about 5'3". He was somewhat overweight. He had hair a little like Larry from the "Three Stooges," and he spoke with a distinct lisp. Not quite what I had expected. Within seconds, however, I was drawn to the unique style that Ben Feldman possessed. He had none of the more conventional strengths that we associate with his kind of success, yet he was dominant in his field.

Then and there, I learned the most valuable lesson I had ever learned about personal style. I could not be Ben Feldman; I could, however, focus on his technique and process. Even more importantly, I was forced to ask myself, "How can I do that so it sounds like Rob Jolles?" What is my personal style? Rob's strengths aren't Ben's strengths. I had to figure out what I could draw upon within myself – things that are uniquely me.

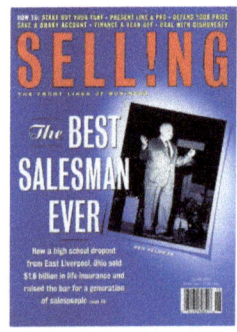

Ben Feldman should be an inspiration to us all. With few to none of the classic attributes we associate with successful salespeople, Ben Feldman committed to his own, unique style, and sold 1.6 *billion* dollars of insurance in his lifetime! Each of us possesses our own, unique style. The key to being a good salesperson, or whatever you choose to do, is not only learning what that natural style is, but committing to it.

Can anybody sell? *Absolutely!* You just have to separate style from technique. Unfortunately, sales managers and sales trainers often preach more of their style than their technique, and the predictable, disappointing results speak for themselves.

Not a Blog ~ Not an Article ~ A Blarticle®

In the summer of 1994, Ben Feldman passed away, but he left us a few final gifts. He left many process behaviors that are repeatable and effective when working with clients. I think his greatest gift, however, may have been one he never articulated. He taught us all that if you commit to your own personal style, and truly commit to it, there is no limit to how successful you can become!

I'll admit it. As a salesman, and sales trainer, for over two decades I was firmly convinced that the only way to motivate a person to accept change was through having him or her examine the consequences of not doing so. I still think it's the most powerful approach, but it's not the only approach. I'll show you both approaches with you read...

The Two Ways to Motivate Others

How many times have you thought to yourself, "If I could just reach in and motivate that person things would be a lot easier." This is your lucky week because in this short blog, I think I can provide you with some awfully useful information that will start you on your path to motivating others. In fact, when it comes down to it, there are really only two ways to motivate others. People are motivated by consequence or value. That's not debatable. What is debatable is exactly how to figure out which is appropriate for the person you are communicating with.

For example, your typical cigarette smoker will stop smoking for one of two reasons. They might quit because it begins to dawn on them just how much money they might save, and what they could do with that money – value. Or, they may stop because of a health scare they hear from a friend, or even from their own doctor – consequence. Even in this example, you can see that consequence is often the more powerful motivator, but let's save that for another blog. The fact is that it often comes down to learning what motivates each unique individual.

Consequence is seen through the eyes of another as, "What will happen if I *don't* make a change?" Value is seen through the eyes of another as, "What will happen if I *do* make a change?" It would make things much easier if people showed up with a user's manual and told you which motivation they subscribed to, but it doesn't work that way. We have to figure it out on the fly.

If you want to speak someone else's language, it is awfully important to determine what motivates them to action. I want to start by encouraging you to remember: It's not what motivates *you* – it's what motivates the person you are communicating with. How many times have you bought someone a gift you thought he or she was going to love, but you realized later that it was *you* who loved that item. This same kind of blindness takes place when we motivate others, and we have to be wary of it.

Let me give you a couple of ideas to help you figure this out. Anyone who has ever spent a minute with me already knows any conversation begins with questions. The more someone else talks, the more they typically like us. It makes sense to begin with easy, non-problem related questions, such as: "What brought you into this business?" You will probably hear one of two answers:

- "I always wanted to work for myself. I just couldn't stand putting in the hours for someone else's profit." This reflects a decision based on consequence.
- "I always wanted to work for myself. I enjoy spending time with people and working with their families." This reflects a decision based on value.

Quite simply, if you hear a response filled with concerns that needed to be addressed, you are working with someone who makes decisions based on consequences. If you hear a response that paints a more pleasant picture of change, you are working with someone who makes decisions based on value. You can choose questions that mirror the appropriate approach, drilling down into the *consequence* of not making a change, or the *value* of making that change. As you dig deeper into the conversation, you can use questions to fit the person, such as:

- "I always wanted to work for myself. I just couldn't stand putting in the hours for someone else's profit."

"How many hours a week were you putting in?"

- "I always wanted to work for myself. I enjoy spending time with people and working with their families."

"What are some of the other benefits you get from working for yourself?"

By understanding what motivates people and learning how to determine these qualities in those you are conversing with, you can structure your conversation to support this. This knowledge will go a long way in helping you to connect, at a much deeper level, with those you are communicating with. It's just a matter of speaking the other person's language… so to speak!

I was never the greatest chess player, but I sure have become a fan of the clock they use to time their games. That obscure little device can provide a unique approach to measuring how effectively we communicate. I'll tell you exactly how, and why when you read…

Want to Measure Your Sales Aptitude? Try Using a Chess Clock

It's common knowledge that the art of effective communication lies in our ability to ask questions and listen. I'm sure I didn't just tell you something you haven't heard before, but why is it so many people struggle with this simple concept?

For years, I've tried to reinforce the necessity of asking questions. I've gone so far as to carry tape recorders to my seminars just to prove to people that they are not asking as many questions as they may think. The exercise is this: I ask people to pair up, and each take five minutes trying to sell something to each other. I tell them that it is merely an exercise to monitor their particular communication style, but it is actually an exercise in counting the number of questions the other is asking.

When the exercise has been completed, we talk about the importance of asking questions. The students go back and count the number of statements versus the number of questions and return with a ratio.

Ideally, I'm hoping for a 1:1 ratio, but in reality, anything around three statements for every question or under is acceptable. That ratio allows us to track the percentage of time those we are communicating with are talking versus the percentage of time *we* are talking.

I've come to realize that although the exercise provides some strong indicators of success, the exercise is flawed for two reasons. First, too many questions may be worse than no questions at all. There are those individuals who proudly announce that they have asked 30 questions. That's thirty questions… in five minutes! Sounds pretty intense to me. Was that a conversation or an interrogation? We're not using questions as a weapon; merely a way to engage others in conversation. A ratio like this indicates the overuse of questions that require a "yes" or "no" response, or what is commonly referred to as closed questions. Imagine a conversation that went like this:

- "Hi. It's nice to finally meet you. Do you like this restaurant?"
- "Yes."
- "Are you hungry?"
- "Yes, uh, yes I am."
- "Isn't the weather warm this time of year?"
- "Oh yes, uh, it's really warm!"

We could let a conversation like that continue painfully, and it would score well in our statements versus questions ratio, but it could hardly be viewed as an effective conversation. Closed questions might be a great way to confirm information, or to test understanding, but it is not the way to warm up a conversation.

But the bigger problem seems to affect those who are actually doing far better than the ratio might indicate. We want to make it comfortable for the other person to respond to our questions. Questions that can't be answered with a "yes" or "no" are referred to as open questions, and they are typically used to help open up a more reserved individual, or to help others to expand on the information being provided. Early in a conversation, open questions are wonderful when the conversation has the potential to be the most awkward. Imagine a conversation that goes like this:

- "Hi. It's nice to finally meet you. Everyone has a story. I'd love to hear yours."
- "Yes… I mean, well, it's funny that I'm even here to today. I never thought I'd leave my hometown, but as they say, sometimes you don't find your career; it finds you. I was working for a small company when one day…"

Now, let's go back to that classic exercise to measure communication effectiveness that counts the number of questions being asked. With the use of multiple open questions, that classic ratio might be somewhat unbalanced, but is the conversation itself unbalanced? The answer is no, and that's why I have become such a big fan of chess clocks.

A typical chess clock has two buttons and two clocks. When these clocks are used to measure a conversation, I have students use one clock to measure the amount of time they are talking and the other to measure the amount of time the other person is talking. At the end of a role-play, the students are left with a much more accurate measurement of who is doing most of the talking. Now a 1:1 time ratio really means something!

How do you keep your questions open, and thereby allow others to speak freely? If you start a sentence with words like "tell, describe, what, why, and how," your questions will be open. On the flipside, if you start your sentences with words like "do, are, is, if, or can," your questions will be closed, and the responses will be choppy and short. Mark Twain once said:

"The difference between the almost right word and the right word is really a large matter - 'tis the difference between the lightning bug and the lightening."

Rob Jolles

All you really need to do is focus on the first word out of your mouth and you'll not only be using the right word, but you'll also be building the right question. Who knew such a simple device could provide such an accurate indicator of how well we communicate with others?[1]

---

1. I got a little carried away with this one, and broke the 750-word... usually rule. It happens now and then!

W hat if I told you that there is one question that you can ask that will tell you more about a person than any other question you'll ever ask. You'll hear all about it when you read…

Everybody Has a Story…

There are few things that are indisputable when trying to learn about another individual. It all begins with trust. Here's what I know to be true:

- No one is going to open up to another individual if they don't trust him or her.
- Trust is earned.
- Trust is earned by asking questions, and listening.
- The questions that are asked must be sincere, and must allow individuals to tell "their story."

I recently had a conversation with my buddy Bubba, a salesman whom I've known for over twenty years. He is one of the best salesmen I've ever met. We were talking about questions we can ask that help to build trust between people, and questions that allow us to learn volumes about another person. He shared a question that I found to be the best question I've ever come across.

Now, before I present you with the best question I've ever come across, I should probably mention the two characteristics of a very good question.

First, it should be an open question. Open questions are questions that cannot be answered with a simple "yes" or "no." When asking questions and trying to create trust, we are not "interrogating" another individual. Open questions require a more thoughtful response from those who are answering it, and the more someone talks, the more they like the person they are talking to.

Second, it should be a question that did not involve a particular problem. Don't get me wrong, at some point we will ask questions that are not as comfortable to answer, but those questions have to wait until trust has been established.

So we know that if we are going to use questions to create trust, those initial questions are critical. That's why the simplicity and effectiveness of the following question, resonated so deeply within me. The question was this:

"Everyone has a story. I'm interested in listening to yours."

You would be amazed at where that question can lead. The answer to that particular question can provide an instant window into another person's personality, just by the depth of his or her response. The answer to that question can provide information that someone may rarely tell another individual. The truth is that people *want* to tell other people their story. The beauty of this question is that it's non-threatening to the people you're asking; they can answer with as much or as little depth as they feel comfortable.

The next time you are in a situation where you really want to get to know another person, and you want to begin to create trust, ask that question. Then settle back, and listen carefully. There's no telling where the story might end up, but conversation will end in a deeper level of trust. Thanks Bubba.

Want to find out who is responsible for making purchase decisions? You can't ignore the person you're speaking to, but you want to speak to the decision maker. You have to be careful in how you word this question, and you'll see what I mean when you read…

Asking Almost the Right Question

There are a number of important questions that every salesperson must ask. Some of these questions involve gaining a commitment to change, the clarification of objections, earning the client's trust, or even creating urgency. Some questions involve a final commitment to actually making a commitment. But there's one other question that comes very early in the conversation, and it can lead to either a great talk or a waste of time.

The question I'm referring to involves the confirmation that you are actually speaking to the right person. Often, this question is asked in a closed and flawed manner. Let me provide you with an example: You are meeting with a new client for the first time, and early on in the conversation, you need to make sure you are talking with the right person. You ask this question:

"Will you be the person who is in charge of making this purchase decision?"

It doesn't get much easier than that, does it? You asked in a simple, straightforward, and yet, terribly flawed way. I can't tell you how many times I've been told by sales people: "I ask my prospects if they are the decision makers, they tell me they are, and then, later in the process, I realize they aren't! I can't do more than ask!" In fact, it's a case of asking *almost* the right question.

When I was 21 years old and in my first week working for New York Life, I remember a day when the Canon copier rep came in to try to sell us new office copiers. I could not have been lower on the totem pole in the company, but I was the one asked to meet with this sales rep to hear his or her pitch. I was fully prepared to spend as little time with him or her as possible, when there was a knock at my door, and in walked one of the most attractive women I had ever seen. In that I was young, single, and human, I remember being asked *almost* the right question:

"Will you be the person who is charge of making this purchase decision?"

With a slight crack in my voice, my libido / ego forced me to answer her question in a proud but dishonest way: "Yes, I am," and therein lies the problem with asking *almost* the right question. When you ask people if they are the ones in charge of making the decisions, you force them to be dishonest. Imagine if I had given the real answer to her question: "No, I'm not the person in charge of making this or any decisions here at this office. As a matter of fact, I'm pretty much the low man on the totem pole here. Hey, would you like to go out and catch a movie sometime?"

So now that we've taken a look at asking *almost* the right question, let's move a few words around and make it the right question. If you want to find out who is in charge of making a purchase decision, why not ask the question this way:

"Who, besides yourself, will be responsible for making this purchase decision?"

It's just a word or two, but by changing the question in this way, you are allowing the people involved to provide an honest answer without embarrassing themselves or overstating their real positions. Such a simple concept, yet a great example of how the wording of a question can be the key to getting the correct answer. I think Mark Twain said it best:

"The difference between the almost right word & the right word is really a large matter - it's the difference between the lightning bug and the lightning."

W e're taught to persuade by learning to ask questions and listen. But there's another lesson that is quickly forgotten, and you'll get a gentle reminder when you read…

Is It a Conversation or an Interrogation?

So much has been written about the need to ask questions. Sometimes I feel guilty reminding people how important it is to ask questions. Need I remind you that the more people talk, the more they like the person they are talking to? I guess not. Should I remind you that asking questions indicates that you are really interested in the person you're talking to? I suppose not. Lastly, have I mentioned that asking questions is crucial in building trust? Darn it; there I go again! But what if I told you that's only half the story?

In some of the workshops I deliver, I run a little exercise that involves having people take turns selling something to another individual. I pass out small tape recorders so they can record those conversations. By listening to the recordings, we find that they may not be asking any questions or believe it or not, they are asking too many questions.

Is it possible to actually ask too many questions? It sure is, particularly if you are asking the wrong kind of questions. The right kind of questions are open questions: questions that cannot be answered with a simple "yes" or "no." Open questions get people to expand on information, and they can open up a reserved person. Sometimes, a well placed open question like, "Everybody has a story; what's yours?" can take another person five minutes to answer.

On the other hand, closed questions are questions that *can* be answered with a simple, "yes" or "no." They can confirm information, test understanding, and sometimes intimidate another individual. Closed questions not only don't get a conversation going, and they can kill a good conversation.

I think everyone has a memory of a bad first date with someone, and I'm guessing that there were a lot of closed questions asked during those dates. The conversation may have been like this:

- "So, uh, you lived here long?"
- "Uh, yes, I sure have."
- "Hmm. That's nice. Uh, do you like sushi?"
- "Uh, yes, yes I do."
- "Hmm."

I could go on but it's too painful. Closed questions not only kill a good conversation, but they also can intimidate. If you've ever been stopped by a police officer for speeding, I'm guessing you didn't hear many open questions like, "How you doing sir – share with me your feelings about the laws in this great state of Maryland?" Instead, you most likely heard:

- "Do you know why I pulled you over?"
- "Do you understand the laws in this state?"
- "Do you have your license and registration for that vehicle?"

This isn't an accident. These questions are intended to intimidate you. This is not supposed to be a conversation; it's an interrogation, and it's quite effective if you are a police officer!

You see, just learning to ask questions is not enough. You need to know what kinds of questions to ask, and when to ask them. By doing that, you'll learn a lot about the person you're talking to and the conversation will flow effortlessly. It is such a seemingly simple concept, but being aware of the kinds of questions you ask will serve you well.

If you want to influence the action of others, you need to study the process others go through when they consider change. Within that process is one, crucial decision point that is an **A**chilles' heel for so many of us. You'll understand just how important this issue can be when you read…

The Line in the Sand

Some years ago, my wife and I owned a Mercury Marquis that was one, interesting piece of work. It was a fine car, but we had it for quite some time, and over the years it developed some rather interesting, uh, habits. It had a rattle of some sort in the back wheel, but we got used to it. The dashboard light had a mind of its own and would come on and off on its own schedule, but we got used to it. It had a ding here, and some rust there, and the mileage wasn't quite what we had in mind, but we got used to it. In fact, there were a lot of nagging issues with this car, and we mumbled from time to time that we should probably get rid of it, but that was just idle chatter.

Then one day the car surprised us with a new interesting habit. Early one morning we drove to a friend's house in a quiet little suburban neighborhood in Maryland and as we turned into the neighborhood the horn went off all by itself. As soon as we completed our turn into the neighborhood the horn stopped. Mortified, we continued on. A couple of blocks later we turned again, and again that horn with an apparent mind of its own went off again. Quickly, we completed the turn and it stopped again. As luck would have it we had to make at least four more turns, and each time we took a turn, that horn let all within ear shot know we were on their street.

When we finally reached our friend's house and announced our arrival to the dozens of neighbors, we no doubt woke up, we were clear on two things. First, we needed to cut the wire to that car horn. Second, we needed to say goodbye to this car. We had crossed that line in the sand between not liking something, and deciding to do something about it. We had made a commitment to change.

When it comes to making decisions, it's clear that we go through repeatable, predictable stages. However, within this cycle there is one, significant, moment of truth that seems to be missed by many, and yet, is vital to those who seek to change minds. In a sense, it represents a line in the sand.

I am in no way a cynic, but I am a realist. These two things I know to be true:

- It is human nature to spend months, if not years, living with problems we are capable of fixing… but we just don't. We wait until these problems become big problems, and change often comes too late.
- It is human nature to fear change, and that fear can be so blinding that we can't see size and scope of problems until there is a difficult, if not devastating, scenario.

We live with these problems, we justify these problems, we whine about these problems, we sulk about these problems, we turn away and we even deny these problems exist. And then something happens.

That something can be as simple as a comment that catches us by surprise, and other times it can be as lethal as firing at work, but something happens. When that something happens, we cross a line I've nicknamed, "The fix, don't fix line" and in a sense, it is mythical line in the sand. When we cross that line, we don't commit to a solution; we commit to a change.

- We can complain about an unfulfilling job for years. We've crossed that line in the sand when we have a resume redone and begun networking
- We can complain about an unfulfilling relationship for years. We've crossed that line in the sand when we find ourselves a therapist and set an appointment.
- We can complain about a car that has too many miles on it. We've crossed that line in the sand when we find ourselves pulling into a dealership.

There are moments of truth in all our lives. These moments of truth frequently initiate change. Personally, I'd rather help someone avoid a catastrophe, then help someone clean one up, and that's why this line in the sand is so important to me. Understanding this line helps to remind me how important it is to help others navigate this line. It's not unusual to struggle with change; we all do. What is unusual is for people, on their own, to fix these problems before it's too late.

During any conversation that involves influence or persuasion, there is the need to ask difficult questions. Sometimes, those questions can lead to trouble, which can lead to an inspired moment, and you'll see just what I mean when you read…

A Most Unusual Nickname

Through our lives, we may be called a nickname or two. I had plenty of them. When I was five years old, my hair was very short, and spikey, and my dad called me "bur head." If it came from my dad, it was alright by me. I was called "Broadway" in high school, "Peppy" in college, and "The Rocket" in business. But at a financial conference in San Antonio, in front of an audience of almost 1,000 people, I was called a nickname that threw me, but only for a moment or two.

It was an exciting event with an impressive group of professional speakers huddled together in the green room behind the stage. Normally at a conference like this, one or two professionals would be hired to speak. At this conference, eight speakers were each given one-hour slots to wow the audience. If that doesn't get your heart beating, you need to get your ticker checked. It was in that green room, while I was watching the speaker before me on the monitor, that I heard my new nickname. It started innocently enough…

"Today you're going to hear from many great speakers, but there's one in particular who I'm not that fond of. He believes you need to not just uncover an issue that a client may be protecting; he believes you need to continue to get that client to talk about this issue, which he sometimes calls a wound. I call a person like this person a scab picker."

A hush fell over the green room where the remaining speakers and I were sipping on water, making idle chatter, and watching the monitor. There were some rather humorous and quizzical looks as if each was saying, "That's not me - is it you?" I smiled and said, "I think that's me" and began to get mic'd up for my rebuttal... I mean presentation.

So many thoughts raced through my head as I stood off stage waiting for my *real* name to be called. But within seconds, I knew what I wanted to say. When my name was called and I walked towards the microphone, I was ready...

"Ladies and gentlemen, my name is Rob Jolles, and I am a scab-picker. I know that might sound like a terrible name, but I am not ashamed of it. I'm proud of it. You see, I know that people do not instinctively fix small problems; they fix big problems. What's more, I know that the fear of the unknown often outweighs the pain of the present.

So, what can we do about it? We have two choices: The first is to ignore it, and hope it goes away. Ignore it? I've spent most of my professional career observing the tragedy that falls on those we care about because no one has the courage to step forward and ask difficult questions. It can be as simple as poor study habits, or as complicated as a dysfunctional scar stemming from a troubled childhood. The players change, and certain elements of the plot change, but the results are the same. In the end, there's the feeling that there's nothing we can do about it. We can't ignore it.

My other option is to try and do something about it. Doing something about it begins by creating trust, and then earning the right to actually have someone tell you about a particular problem. That can be uncomfortable, and that's not even half the job. If you believe in the change you are trying to create, you have to be willing to get your hands dirty. Getting your hands dirty means asking more questions about the pain someone might be trying to avoid. It means opening the wound a bit more. For the lack of a better word, it means being a scab-picker. That's what I believe, that's what I teach, and that's who I am."

It was a rather shocking opening to a presentation, and not a nickname I'd like to put on my luggage tag, but I stand by those words. The next time you are nose-to-nose with another individual who desperately needs to change their ways, I hope you remember these words as well.

It's a stumbling block for all of us, but sometimes we have to ask questions that are going to make another person feel pain. But rather than feeling badly about asking those questions, you need to believe in something bigger, and you'll see what I mean when you read….

Asking Disturbing Questions - Is it Mean, or is it Merciful?

There's no sugarcoating it: The most challenging part of the job of a salesperson, a parent, or of anyone who wants to persuade, is to ask the more difficult questions. These are the questions that are sometimes referred to as "pain" questions. If you spend two weeks in a sales training class, you know that it all comes down to one thing: Can you create pain without creating conflict?

I recently received an email from a salesperson I know; I have coached this person and I also deeply respect her. In her email, she told me that she had just asked some of those "pain" questions to a client, and successfully, I might add. The process of forcing her client to look at the most difficult aspects of his resistance to change, however, made her "feel a little mean."

Those four words made me stop what I was doing, take a deep breath, and swallow hard. At that moment, I had to accept the fact that I wasn't doing my job. I had failed to teach this person the most important lesson I could ever teach her. When you force someone to answer a difficult question - a question that makes another person feel the pain of not taking action, you are not being aggressive. You are, in fact, being empathetic.

I'll go a step further. I firmly believe it's one of the sincerest acts of kindness you can offer another human being. We've all seen people who are struggling at home, or at work, and we want to help them. Anyone can come to the rescue with his or her wonderful ideas on what another person should do. It never creates change, but it's a comfortable conversation. I'm talking about taking the tougher road, but ultimately, the much more successful road.

It hurts to be asked by another person what room the children are in when they are fighting with their spouse, but the answer can lead a couple to therapy. It hurts to be asked what impact not supporting a corporate directive could have on a new, starry-eyed manager, but the answer can save a career.

I want people to understand that the process of persuasion isn't ruled simply by a tactic. It must be accompanied by an emotion. That emotion is one of empathy. You have to believe in the tough questions you ask, and then you will succeed. You'll succeed in the art of persuasion, and you'll succeed because you are exemplifying the art of caring about another person. When you ask difficult questions, it is never mean. It is compassionate and possibly life changing. Once confronted with the tragedy so many endure because of their inability to make tough decisions on their own, you see that these questions are, in fact, merciful.

In the end, you get to save things. You get to save both people and businesses, because the path you took required discipline and courage. The results you initiated changed another person's life. You were the one who helped someone move past his or her fear of change, and into the future. Doing something like that is never mean. It's quite the contrary. It is something to be proud of.

I'm going to guess that many of you accept the notion that "more" is always better. Some money is good, but "more" is better. After all, one lobster tail is good, but two or three are better. It's good to have a few good friends, but having "more" friends is even better. Ironically, when it comes to persuading others, "more" may create "more" challenges then benefits, and I'll tell exactly what I mean when you read...

When More Is Not Better

Let's face it: We've been raised with the idea that "more" is better. If you really want to see this concept play out in all its glory, watch someone try to persuade someone else. What takes place is fairly predictable. I'm a huge fan of questions, but at some point, in the discussion, the conversation will shift. It will be your turn to make your case. Maybe you'll be making the case as to why your product is the perfect solution for a potential client. Maybe you'll be making the case as to why you are the perfect person to fill a particular job. Maybe the case you'll be making is why the movie or restaurant you are suggesting is the perfect fit for your evening.

So, how do you make your case? If you're like most, you can't wait to present the powerful reason that will persuade and make your case! But then something happens. A thought emerges: If one powerful reason is good, two might be even better. Why stop at two? Three solid reasons must be better, and four will knock the cover off this conversation! And therein lies the problem.

. . .

Think about a time when you were making a point with your children. As a parent, you sat down after dinner to talk about the issue of homework not being turned in on time. You told your child that he or she was not acting in a responsible manner; a note from the teacher turned this into a pretty cut and dry conversation… but you couldn't leave it alone. You were on a roll and so, to strengthen your case about responsibility, you decided to throw in a few other things that go under the category of lack of responsibility: "You're not practicing your trumpet, you're not putting your things away, and you're not completing your chores." "More" might seem better until you hear this: "I just finished washing the dishes two hour ago!" You're left sputtering along with a nervous attempt to get back on track: "Uh, well, you see, that's not really what we are talking about…" Do you still think "more" is better?

We are drawn to the idea that 'more" is better, when the reality is that "more" is anything but better.

- "More" can actually dilute your own argument. Remember, there is usually a very compelling case that you are putting forth. "More" reasons to support your original argument really means "less important reasons" and those less important reasons could very well be the undoing of your original argument.
- "More" can actually make you vulnerable to your own argument. As you pile the less important ideas into the case you are making, it's not uncommon to end up talking about things that aren't important to you or the person you are talking to. Want to witness an awkward moment? Watch someone bring up a reason to support an idea, and then be challenged on that particular unimportant point. You'll see that person try to un-bring it up, but it's too late; his or her own words have already set the trap!
- "More" can actually reduce your credibility. We live in an

environment that covets quick communication. The longer it takes to prove a point, the more suspect that point becomes.

Once again, it becomes a case of instinct versus logic. On many levels, it feels instinctively right to provide as many reasons as possible to win that argument, prove a point, or make a case. "More" may *feel* better, but it ends up being illogical. You may be proud of the extra examples that you've stuffed into your argument, but ultimately, those examples can be the cause of your undoing. When you let logic rule the day, you'll find that your most compelling argument is far easier to state and defend than a series of less important clutter.

More may seem better in many situations, but not when it comes to arguing your case a simple proverb sums it up the best: "Don't use a lot where a little will do."

Want to have a better understanding of what truly motivates people when they are looking to buy? You'll get that answer, *and* one of my favorite poems when you read…

Don't Sell Me Things

When I was recently working with a group of sales professionals, a discussion broke out that represented an interesting moment of truth. I was trying to convince this group that they were too caught up in the features of the product they were selling. I was trying to convince this group that these products, these "things," weren't as important as they thought.

But this group seemed a bit insulted, and they took great pride in their products. They didn't like hearing that they were selling me "things." I tried to explain to them that people don't want to be sold "things." They want to be to sold what these "things" represent. As I tried to explain to them that I needed to hear the *value* of their product, they tried to elaborate on the intricacies of the *features* of their product. I finally had heard enough, and I reached for my secret weapon.

My secret weapon is a poem that had been given to me about 25 years ago. It came from a 1941 Sears sales publication, and its timeless message dealt with the exact concept I was trying to explain to these sales professionals in our 2012 world. It clarified the difference between a "thing" – with all of its many features, and a benefit of that "thing." After you read this poem, you'll understand…

Don't Sell Me Things

Don't sell me clothes. Sell me a neat appearance, style, and attractiveness.

Don't sell me shoes. Sell me foot comfort and the pleasure of walking in the open air.

Don't sell me candy. Sell me happiness and pleasure of taste.

Don't sell me furniture. Sell me a home that has comfort, cleanliness and convenience.

Don't sell me books. Sell me pleasant hours and the profit of knowledge.

Don't sell me toys. Sell me playthings to make my children happy.

Don't sell me tools. Sell me the pleasure and profit of making fine things.

Don't sell me refrigerators. Sell me the health and better flavor of fresh foods.

Don't sell me tires. Sell me freedom from worry and low cost per mile.

Don't sell me plows. Sell me green fields of waving wheat.

Don't sell me things. Sell me ideas, feelings, self-respect, home life, happiness. Please, don't sell me things.

If you ever come to my office, you'll see some interesting things on the wall. I'm very proud of the pictures, the book covers, the various mementos, and a few other things I hope will motivate the people who come to visit. What they don't see are the few things that are taped on the back panel of my desk that only *I* can see. These are the items that motivate me. I have this trusty poem in a prime location on that back panel, and every time I read it, I appreciate the simple wisdom in those words. I hope you do too.

Performance

This section of the book focuses on performance, and explores what it truly takes to deliver at the highest level—whether in presentations, leadership, or personal growth. It uncovers the effort behind seemingly effortless success, the role of preparation under pressure, and the fine balance between confidence and humility. Here you'll explore the psychology of effective communication, and why authenticity matters more than perfection. With lessons on resilience, motivation, this section serves as a guide to mastering performance in both professional and personal arenas.

What does a comedy team – the greatest comedy team *ever* – have to do with the way you present information? Everything! I'll tell you who they are, why you should care, and even a secret connection I have with these amazing two men when you read…

The Perfect Performance Combination

Question: Who do you think were the comedians in the greatest comedic team ever to step on a stage? To me, there is one, simple answer: Jerry Lewis and Dean Martin. Do you want to debate this with me? You won't stand a chance. Consider the following facts:

- These two performers had the number one TV show – The Colgate Comedy Hour.
- These two performers had the number one Radio show – The Dean Martin & Jerry Lewis Radio Show.
- These two performers had the number one movie – The Caddy.
- These two performers had the number one song – "That's Amore."
- These two performers had the number one nightclub act; They performed *five* shows a day at the Atlantic City's 500 Club.

Pretty impressive, huh? Now, what if I told you that every accomplishment you just read happened simultaneously? Together, their success was unrivaled, and yet individually, they were each forgettable. While Dino Paul Crocetti was struggling as a nightclub singer, Joseph Levitch was struggling with a comedy act in which he lip-synched to records. But when they linked up, they created a performance chemistry that I believe will never be duplicated again. However, the formula that they followed that lead to their success is something that can be duplicated.

Dean was the stability. He was the voice of reason that reached out and made you care. But too much reason can bore an audience, and put them to sleep. Jerry was the energy. He was the spark that reached out and grabbed your attention. But too much energy can overwhelm an audience and wear them out. Together they created performance magic because the combination of stability and energy left audiences breathless. They were the perfect combination.

Now think about how you present material in a presentation you're giving. You need the stability that Dean represented. You need that voice of reason. That comes through in the information you present. No audience wants to sit through a presentation that consists solely of stories, poems, and jokes, but provides little actual information.

Of course, you need that energy that Jerry represented too. You need that spark. That comes through in the interest sustaining ideas you weave into your presentation, such as humor, mobility, and various presentation aids. No audience wants to sit through a presentation that grinds on and on, and overwhelms attendees with too much information. But when you can put the information and energy together, you have the perfect combination.

This is a message I take very seriously, so seriously I carry a private little reminder with me every time I step on a stage. Fourteen years ago, I stumbled across an online auction that was selling a pair of Jerry and Dean cufflinks. In 1954, Paramount Pictures was releasing their newest movie, "Living it Up," and they produced 150 of these cufflinks as a promotion. I jumped in on this auction and I bought those cufflinks for a reason: I wanted that reminder with me each and every time I stepped in front of an audience.

The next time you see me on stage, you might want to come on up and ask to take a look at these special cufflinks. It will be no coincidence that you will always find Jerry, and that energy, on my left wrist. I happened to be left-handed, and that's where my power comes from. But Dean, and that voice of reason, is on my right. Without him, I'm just a guy who makes people laugh without any real substance. Ah, but when I put the two together and establish that perfect combination, the performance and message can become unforgettable...

The reward for working hard at anything is making what you do look easy to others. Of course, we all know a lot of work goes into making the tasks we perform look simple. If you're looking to make what you do look easy, I'll provide you with three good reminders to focus on when you read…

The Effort Behind Effortless

One of the kindest comments that can come from those we work for is this: "You make what you do look effortless." It doesn't matter if you are a professional speaker, a salesman, a butcher, a baker, or a candlestick maker; when anyone hears that phrase, it can't help but make you feel like you've done your job well. Although our jobs are often anything but easy, it is often our job to make what we do look effortless.

The irony is, the more effort we put behind a task, the more effortless we make the task appear.

Although we all want to make what we do appear simple, it takes work, and lots of it. I'd suggest focusing on these three techniques:

1. Repetition. Like hearing the words, "location, location, location" when we're looking for a new house, making the tasks we perform appear effortless often comes down to, "repetition, repetition, repetition." Repetition is the answer for those seeking to appear effortless and comfortable in his or her skin.
2. Trial and Error. If repetition is the secret sauce to making something appear effortless, trial and error is the spice that adds flavor. What good is making something that is stale, or

clearly not your best, look effortless? The key is not to be afraid of testing and tweaking what you do.
3. Discipline. It takes self-control to do something over and over again. It takes self-restraint to resist the urge to tweak something because *you* are becoming bored with it. When you can apply discipline to both, you move closer to the goal of effortless.

Don't confuse doing something that appears effortless to others with doing something that isn't valued by others. Performing a challenging task, and making it look easy, makes what you do not only relatable, but admired.

Performing a task in an effortless manner requires a journey with no real finish line, and the work that isn't seen is usually what pays the biggest dividends. Through repetition, trial and error, and good old-fashioned discipline, you'll be making the difficult job look effortless in no time!

When you watch a professional presenter perform under pressure, it appears effortless. What you don't see is what goes on *before* that performance, and the way the speaker uses those final few minutes before he or she begins to speak. I'll tell you about my personal ritual, and how this might help you the next time you have to perform under pressure when you read…

Running Your Race

There is no debating the fact that standing before a room full of people creates pressure. The studies continue to point out that fear of heights, snakes, drowning, and needles still round out the top five biggest fears. Still, those fears do not compare to the fear of public speaking. We all deal with the pressure of public speaking. Some people excel  under pressure, and others tend to wither and weaken under the weight of it. We often read about tips and ideas that help to battle this difficult nemesis during a presentation, but personally, I believe the battle is won before the presentation is ever delivered.

Clearly, repetition is the greatest friend of anyone who performs in front of others. The more we perform, the easier it becomes. But even repetition can create problems for performers because we are often lured into complacency. Do you really want to avoid *any* anxiety before an important meeting or presentation? I happen to look forward to that slight, uneasy feeling before a presentation. As a matter of fact, the only time I do feel any sense of real nervousness is when I feel nothing before a presentation. There's an ominous feeling in the air that this might be the day I perform flatly.

The fact is this: We want that pressure; we need that pressure, and it's that pressure that makes us unforgettable. We know that this pressure will abate once we get a few minutes into our presentation, so it's those first few minutes that are the roughest. Unfortunately, that's when the audience is judging us the hardest. When I train speakers, I work hard on working out those first few minutes of delivery, but if pressure gets in the way, the powerful opening is lost. That's why I focus so hard on what happens *before* a presentation is delivered. Consider these four simple thoughts to help you manage this, or for that matter, any pressure situation.

1. Show up early... I mean, early! It never ceases to amaze me when I see someone show up thirty minutes before a presentation and then he or she begins to set up. The pros will show up an hour before a presentation. I show up significantly earlier for a host of reasons: I might have a microphone to work with, or I might be filmed, or I'll need to coordinate audio visuals, or I'll need to test audio levels off my laptop, or I'll be looking to see if there are any audio hotspots that could create feedback, or I'll need to make sure handouts are ready for distribution or, well, you can see that an hour is not early enough. Even if you can work out all of the logistical issues in an hour, it's not early enough for the mental preparation for the presentation.

2. Prepare the mind. It's not uncommon for there to be a lot going on before a presentation. The client often has questions, audience members often wander up with questions, and there are support people who often want to chat. Before you know it, your name is called, and your presentation begins. Is that really the way you want to start your "race?" You show up hours early so, at least 15 minutes before a presentation begins, you don't have to worry about answering any more questions. Find a quiet area where there's a comfortable chair or take a nice, easy walk so you can clear your mind of all distractions.

3. Visualize. It's difficult for me to tell you exactly what to visualize because it really depends on you. Many will visualize those first steps in front of the room, and or seeing themselves successfully accomplishing the task at hand. As for me, I have a mental image of that of a racehorse getting ready to run a race. In my mind, I am walking myself slowly around a mental paddock; quiet, and at peace, relishing the thought of the race that's soon to follow.

4. Be grateful. Five minutes or so before a presentation, wander back into the room, and make sure that those who are running the meeting see you there. If you can, take a position behind the audience. One of the last thoughts I'd suggest you place in your mind is a simple one. Look at the back of those heads and remind yourself to be grateful. Sometimes there will be 20 heads, sometimes 200 heads, and sometimes 2,000 heads. The number is irrelevant. Be grateful that you have a rare, and precious opportunity to be heard. At this moment in time, that audience is there to listen to you. The audience is not your opponent, but rather a gift.

When placed under pressure, we get caught up in so many unnecessary worries that are usually not under our control. Why create even more stress by taking your mind to a negative place? Preparation is the secret weapon and not just preparation for the presentation, but also preparation for that time before the presentation. Properly prepared, doesn't it make sense to take it to a positive place? Just remind yourself that these are the moments in life that make us feel alive. That's something you can control! Enjoy your race.[1]

---

1. I broke the 750-word… usually rule again, but it was worth it!

The world of acting and the world of presenting frequently cross paths. It was the director of a show who taught me a fundamental and invaluable approach to preparation. It may have been the best piece of advice I have ever heard, and it pertains to the preparation for *any* presentation. I'll tell exactly what it is when you read…

Looking to Nail Your Next Presentation? Lock it Down

I'll never forget one of the best directors I ever worked with. He not only believed in me as an actor, but he also believed in my ability to experiment with the role I was given. His shows were legendary, but his success was by design, and not by coincidence.

He was methodical in how he directed his shows. He would block a scene, and direct his actors in a careful and defined manner. As actors, we would learn our lines and we would learn exactly where we needed to be on stage. Once he was satisfied that we had mastered his initial directions, he would turn us loose a bit to explore the way we were delivering our lines, and even to question the particular blocking we had been assigned.

He believed in the actor's ability to understand his or her character, and he believed that actors might want to make certain adjustments… up to a point. Therein lay the genius of this director. You see, he knew the following:

- He knew that the initial changes we would make would be based on a deeper understanding of the character we were playing.
- He knew that the harder we worked to perfect our

performance, the more risk we would run of becoming bored with it.
- He knew that once we became bored with a performance, we would be susceptible to confusing that sense of boredom with inadequacy.
- He knew that his actors might become bored with the performance, but no audience, seeing it for the first time, would ever be.

As a result, this director had a rule, and that rule had to be strictly followed. Actors were allowed to experiment with a role *until* they were two weeks away from the first performance. Once we reached that two-week mark, we were given the instructions to "lock it down." Quite simply, that meant that, under no circumstances, were any further changes permitted. I'll bet that sounds kind of harsh to you, but it was one of the secrets to his success as a director, and a major reason why the performances were so powerful.

Repetition is a best friend to any performer, but repetition can also play tricks on the mind. Like a sinister, unwelcome friend, it can whine, plead, and beg for its unsuspecting victim to listen to its voice of unreason. "If you just add a little here, and change a little there, you can make it even better!" Welcome to the biggest mistake an actor can make when he or she is preparing for a show. It is also the biggest mistake that anyone who presents information can make when preparing for a delivery. Never confuse what may feel stale to you - based on the repetition of that part or presentation, with what appears to others as polish.

One can waste huge amounts of time constantly trying new things in a presentation, because what is really needed is the perfecting of the same moves over and over until it becomes almost muscle memory. This, in turn, frees the mind to perform truly in the moment. Is there a greater gift for someone who has to perform under pressure than the freedom to perform in the moment?

Not a Blog ~ Not an Article ~ A Blarticle®

When I consult with any presenter, or when I am working on any presentation I'm going to deliver, I follow the same lessons I learned as an actor. I enjoy the process of creating a presentation, and experimenting with all kinds of nifty little moves. I add and subtract, I tinker here and adjust there, but seven days before a delivery - I *lock it down*. There are no exceptions to this rule, and no matter how appealing any new shiny object of change may appear, it has no effect on me. That's because no matter how tempting that change may appear, I want the confidence and the polish of the delivery I experience by locking it down.

When you lock down a presentation and when you give yourself at least a week of no changes, you are giving yourself the chance to polish your words, polish your audiovisuals, polish your timing, and perhaps most importantly, increase your confidence. You might want to continue to daydream about your delivery, but now your daydreams are not littered with the confusion of thinking about adding a little here, or changing a little there.

There's a time for experimentation, and there's a time to commit to working on what you have. The next time you have to do anything that requires a performance level of preparation, work your tail off to give yourself the best chance for success, and lock it down one week before that "go time." I can promise you; the results will be astonishing.[1]

---

1. Did I just break that 750-word… usually rule again?! Do as I say… not as I do.

How many times, when you have been under pressure, have you thought to yourself; "If I could just calm myself down, I know I would do better!" I might be out of line here, but I think two words will provide a solution to this problem. You'll see what I mean when you read...

A Two-Word Response to Pressure

I was on the phone with a loyal Blarticle® reader from Atlanta, and we started talking about that word I don't like hearing very often; "nervousness." I've already been over my views of eradicating that word from the Dictionary altogether and replacing it with the word, "anxiousness." Yet, it seems that the word keeps coming up in conversation, so let's go deeper here.

Think about the last big job interview you had, or the last big presentation you delivered, or that recent big client appointment you went on, or that important meeting you conducted. What if I told you that there are two words that are the secret to conquering your anxiousness in these situations?

You want proof? My kids could tell you these two words because they've heard me say them on many high stress occasions. All three of my children have completely conquered their anxiety when acting or speaking in public. They not only excel at it, but they look forward to these types of pressure opportunities. These two words have helped them get there, and will continue to lead them to even greater success.

My wife, Ronni, has heard these words too. Ronni was a person who was deathly afraid to give a presentation in public. Now she excels at it, and looks forward to it as well. Two words allow her to continue to excel.

When I consult with clients, it's one of their first concerns: "If I can remain calm, and conquer this anxiety, I think I'll do well. How do you remain calm under pressure?" The two words are... "Track record."

Not every moment of our lives reflects a track record of success, but there are plenty to draw from. When you can ask yourself, "What usually happens when I'm in a situation like this?" and the answer is "good things," you have a lot less to be anxious about. The anxiety dissipates, and you're able to focus on the task at hand, whether it is an interview, or a presentation, or a client appointment, or a meeting.

If you listen to professional athletes, they'll often tell you how they visualize getting a hit before they swing the bat, or making a basket before they release a shot. They don't get a hit every time, or sink a basket every time they shoot the ball, but their mind is focused on the times they have in the past. That's their track record.

When I clip on a microphone and step on a stage, I'm anxious just like you. You'd think that I wouldn't be, after almost thirty years of doing this, but I am. As a matter of fact, I hope I am, because I plan on channeling that anxiety into energy. If I'm *not* anxious, I do have something to worry about because then I run the risk of being flat.

It's easy to throw out trite statements like, "I plan on channeling that anxiety into energy." However, I can assure you that it is exactly what I plan on doing because I will not be distracted with thoughts of failure or uncertainty. Instead, I'm focused, or should I say comforted, with thoughts of success – previous successes, and that's what we call a track record.

Enough about me: You've had the exact same feelings that I have! Remember your last success – the one where all your hard work paid off, and you thought, "I'm really good at this!" If you were to repeat that same task the next day, you would have a high level of confi-

Not a Blog ~ Not an Article ~ a Blarticle®

dence because you would be basking in your... you guessed it... your track record. Time passes, and we all can get amnesia. We just need to be reminded of our track record from time to time, that's all. It doesn't guarantee success, but it does guarantee that your anxiety will be reduced, if not eliminated, and that makes the task at hand a whole lot easier.

Each time you have success, that track record builds, and so does the byproduct that goes along with it; confidence. The next time you feel a couple of butterflies building up in your belly, make the words, "Track record" your silent mantra and I can promise it will work for you!

What if I can show you how to motivate an audience? I can also help you to dramatically reduce the chances of aggressive behavior from any members of that audience. How? The key is to address one question that is never asked, and I'll show you when and where to do this when you read…

The Most Important Question Rarely Asked

I've often wondered what it would be like to be a schoolteacher. Many people look at professional speakers and corporate trainers as teachers, but there is one critical difference between these two professions. That difference involves the students, and how to motivate them. In school, the motivation is rather simple:

- "Behave or you'll be sent to the principal's office."
- "If you don't pay attention, you won't get a good grade."
- "If you don't get good grades, you won't get into a good school."
- "If you don't get into a good school, you might not get a good job."

In corporate world, the motivation is somewhat different:

- "Pay attention or, I'll send you to… you won't get a… uh, please pay attention!"

Once we leave the hallowed halls of our educational institutions, using fear as a motivator ceases to be effective. Those who choose to be on a stage, a training room, or a conference room, must survive on their own wit and ability to motivate the room.

Sometimes I actually wish a student would stand up, look me in the eye, and say; "I really don't see a need for me to be here. What's in it for me to learn this material?" Does that sound rude or inappropriate to you? I happen to think it's one of the most important questions a student can ask. Don't believe me? Let's look at the alternative.

You walk into a room of ten people. Eight of them really want to hear your message, and they can't wait to listen to what you have to say. Two of them, however, are not happy to be there. Maybe they were forced to go to this meeting by their bosses. Maybe the last time they went to a meeting like this, the presentation was a mess and a total waste of time. Maybe they're just fed up with going to meetings that are of no value to them whatsoever. These people do not walk in with signs saying, "Not Happy to be Here!" Although they're not actually verbalizing this question, they are thinking to themselves: "What's in it for me?" It happens to be the most important question never asked.

It's a shame this was rarely, if ever, modeled in our countless years of education, but let me model it loud and clear right here. Every presentation - I repeat - *every* presentation, should clearly address the benefits of learning what is about to be presented. The presenter needs to answer this question: "What's in it for the student?" What's more, this explanation should come at the very beginning of the presentation.

There's no need take students on a journey that will allow him or her to somehow *discover* the answer to this question. If someone doesn't see value in what you are about to say, why would he or she care what you are going to talk about? Why should they care about who you are, or where your information came from, or what your agenda is? If someone sees value in what you are about to say, he or she will be locked into your talk.

This seems like a good way for all kinds of teachers to begin each and every class. Should teachers do this? Yes. Do the good ones do this? Yes. But in the real world of corporate presentations, when speakers have to manufacture their own motivation, we need to answer the student's question, "What's in it for me?" as early in the presentation as possible. It is one of the most important steps you can take to motivate a room full of attendees, and it will help you to nail the presentation!

When delivering corporate presentations, it's fairly well known that sometime, somewhere early in the presentation every speaker must address what's in it for the audience. The problem is different audience members are motivated by different issues. There is a formula for success that will address all who you speak in front of and I'll tell you what it is when you read...

The Three Levels of Greed

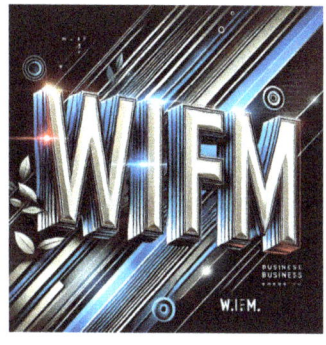

Let's begin by getting past the fifth word in the title of this Blarticle®, which at some level probably offended you. I'm referring to the word, "Greed." But in the words of Gordon Gecko from Wall Street, "Greed is good," and I could not agree more.

Ask yourself why you invested the time to hit the link and read this Blarticle®? Did you feel sorry for me? I'm assuming you've come this far because you felt you could learn some ideas relating to the audiences you might be speaking in front of and you believed this would help you become more successful. I don't want to burst your bubble, but I would call that greed.

No, greed isn't a bad thing. As a matter of fact, I always secretly hope that the audiences I speak in front of are feeling a healthy level of greed. I'm hoping they are practically stewing in their seats thinking, "I sure hope I get something out of this!" This doesn't make me nervous; it inspires me. If I didn't think I had something for that audience, I wouldn't be there. It sure beats the alternative, and that's an audience that slump in their seats thinking, "I couldn't care less if I learn something or not. I just need a place to rest." Not exactly a formula for success for the audience or the unfortunate speaker who address this audience.

So now that we can agree that greed isn't a bad thing, how do we approach this topic with the audience? What isn't debated is the fact that it needs to be addressed as early as possible in the presentation. The real question is *how* to address it. In a perfect world we could survey the audience before we get there and ask them, "What would you like to get out of this presentation?" Unfortunately, this isn't a perfect world, and the closest we usually get is a meeting planner, or manager's version of the response to that question. That's just not good enough, and that's why I have always believed in addressing greed at these three levels:

1. "What's in it for me personally?" This first level of greed comes from a basic need level for us all. On the surface, when we are talking about business issues speakers will tend to miss this one, when in fact the majority of the audience is searching for an answer. It's not unusual for a new skill or an idea that's being taught in business to have personal benefits as well. For example, "Learning this new approach is something you can apply to the way you process the things you do at home."
2. "What's in it for me professionally?" This second level of greed is one that is most commonly addressed, and takes care of a high percentage of the audience. You would be surprised at how many speakers do not address this and merely assume the audience can connect the dots. We all know what happens when we assume! You will never lose an audience member by taking a moment early to address this. An example would be, "In addition, learning this new approach will simplify your day-to-day activities, and provide you with more time to spend with your clients."
3. "What's in it for the company?" The most forgotten level of greed is one that might represent the smallest portion of the audience… but politically, it is often the most important part of the audience. What is the downside of addressing the big picture of your presentation and answering this question?

An example would be, "Ultimately, if we as a company make the cultural shift that's necessary to adopt these new skills, it's going to benefit the company's bottom line, and that's good for everyone."

The reality is, we never know which of these three levels will attract which members of the audience, but collectively we know we satisfy all needs when we begin our presentations this way. We're talking about carefully thinking out about 45 seconds of conversation, and when you do, I can assure you you'll have *everyone's* attention.

It happens to the best of us. You are motoring through a conversation or a presentation, and suddenly something goes awry. The next move you make is a big one, and frequently, it's the wrong one. I'll share with you the right one when you read...

Honesty Is Not Always the Best Policy

I've never been fond of a tattle-tale. I didn't like them when I was a kid, and I don't like them now. Can you imagine the nerve of someone telling on you when you're in an important meeting? Perhaps you're standing in front of an audience, in the middle of a presentation, when the tattle-tale strikes. Talk about nerve! Who, in their right mind, would actually go  out of their way to alert others of a mistake you have made? To make it even worse, it is almost always a mistake no one would actually catch if this knucklehead didn't blab to others around them?! It turns out that this knucklehead is you!

It happens to the best of us. You are in a pressure situation, and under pressure, it isn't unusual for the mouth to be moving faster than the brain can think. Instead of slipping in a filler word like, "um" or "uh," we slip in filler sentences like these:

- "Oh boy, I forgot to bring an important document. That's okay; we can work with this other one instead. It's almost as good anyway."
- "We're running a little short on time today. I'm going to have to cut out a small piece I normally like to do, but we can manage without it."
- "You know I forgot to tell you something I should have mentioned earlier. I'll just tell you about it now."

Unfortunately, these filler sentences are not only unnecessary, but they also alert others of the mistakes you are making. These are mistakes that people would be totally unaware of if there wasn't someone being such a tattletale. You're not just tattling on yourself; you are also diminishing the experience you are creating for others.

- You "forgot to bring an important document?" Just show them the other document that's almost as good, and don't forget it again! Why would you tell them of your mistake? Now you've convinced them that they are receiving inferior information.
- You're "running a little short on time today?" Why do they need to know this information? Cut out that short piece you can easily manage without, and give your audience the joy of being part of a wonderfully run program delivery.
- You "forgot to tell" them something you "should have mentioned earlier?" Just mention it now, and tell them how important it is *to mention it now*. Give them the joy of hearing this essential point.

So often, we are our worst enemies. We aren't being judged on how perfectly we handle information; we are being judged on how perfectly we handle ourselves. For the most part, people are rooting for you. By rooting for you, they are rooting for themselves. They don't need to hear, nor do they *want* to hear, of your mistakes. These mistakes are as irrelevant to them as they are to you. But these filler word phrases, spoken under your breath, are never lost on others. As a matter of fact, these little tattle-tales become a major focus to others and leave a lasting impression. Those you are communicating with are left thinking, "It was a good meeting. If only the person I was listening to had done _____." Mistakes can and will almost always happen.

The next time you are searching for a document, or you're making some delivery decisions on the fly, or you're failing to mention something you normally mention earlier, or you're struggling with any of the thousands of other things that can often go awry, don't be a tattle-tale. Spare all those around you the filler words no one really wants to hear. Just cover it up and push forward!

When we communicate, there is a difference between quality communication and too much communication. This impacts the way we speak, the way we use social media, and even the Blarticle®. You'll see what I mean when you read…

The Art of Making Your Message Stick

While I was conducting a seminar in Connecticut this past week, I was asked a very interesting question by one of the attendees: "When you have a lot information to present, how do you keep the audience focused on the critical information without losing their interest?"

In the world of training, we choose our visual aids wisely. It's been said: "What people hear, they forget. What people see, they remember." Good advice, but what if we put too many visual aids in a presentation? Wouldn't our audience become numb to what they are seeing?

In the world of selling, we choose the benefits of our solution wisely. Benefits reflect specific value to our clients, focusing on exactly what the client wants our solution to do; not what we like best about our solution. If we bury our clients in features that are irrelevant, or advantages that are meaningless, aren't we actually devaluing the recommendation we are making?

That leads me to a rather personal issue. What about how we use social media to communicate with our clients and friends? Facebook, and LinkedIn are wonderful tools, but how many of us have cursed the day when we've accepted a friend request from a good meaning acquaintance? We find out that this acquaintance has decided to use this social media site to inform us of every bike ride, walk in the park, or morsel of food that enters his or her mouth? We move through the stages of frustration, irrelevance, and eventually "hiding" every communication these people post. Sadly, because of the inundation of information, we've shut them out and we may miss an important piece of information they may post.

And therein lies the problem. For 104 weeks in a row, a Blarticle® has appeared faithfully on its website. With well over 1,000 visits a week, this hybrid form of communication has allowed me to reach out and communicate with my friends, clients, colleagues, and countless others.

Fear not! The Blarticle® isn't going anywhere, but after dispensing advice to so many, it's time for me to take my own advice. When we over-communicate, we run the risk of numbing our audience to our message, devaluing our message, and ultimately posting information that will never be seen.

One of the greatest gifts that you, my readers, have given me, are your posts. Those posts tell me that you care, you've connected to a message, and that the message mattered. However, you have not seen the dreaded "unsubscribes" from well-meaning people. They almost always list the same exact reason for their decision to leave - the frequency of delivery. Many of us receive dozens, if not hundreds, of emails in a day. One more email a week, for many, appears to be *too* many. The fact is, posting a weekly Blarticle® creates a risk of over communicating.

Therefore, on this illustrious anniversary, Blarticles® will be posted every other week on an experimental basis. Some have told me: "I wake up on Fridays, and I look forward to reading those Blarticles®!" My response: "Hang in there, grab another cup of coffee, drop by the Blarticle® site, and dig into some Blarticles® from the past. But remember the reason for this change and perhaps you can apply this thought to your world:

"Emphasize everything… emphasize nothing."

Let's face it, there are some people in this world we are destined to *not* get along with. Try as you might, it just isn't meant to be. But sometimes the desire to win over certain people can have disastrous effects on others, and this is never truer than in front of an audience. I'll tell you all about it when you read…

You Can't Hug a Porcupine

One of the unique challenges of delivering workshops is working effectively with the various personalities that populate your audiences. Most workshops tend to last longer, and have smaller crowds, so it's not unusual for there to be a lot of contact between speakers and their audiences. Some participants talk a lot, and some are quiet. Some are funny, and some are not. But some are just not nice, and those porcupines are the ones you need to beware of.

Clearly our goal, as well as our instinct is to get along with everyone. That means if there's a porcupine who isn't particularly pleasant, our reflex is to make sure we do everything we can do to get along swoops in to save the day. That's not just what a presenter does, that's what a leader does, and that's what makes this issue such a difficult one. You see often in this particular situation; our instinct is wrong.

So, is Rob Jolles actually saying to go to battle with all porcupines?! No, but Rob Jolles is saying to not be fooled by thinking the best way to deal with those who aren't pleasant is to kill them with kindness. It just won't work.

First, you risk losing the rest of those who are toeing the line and who you actually want to work with. We've all seen these porcupines that hold a room hostage with his or her inappropriate behavior. The "I'll turn this person around if it's the last thing I do" drive kicks in and the presenter gets to work. They fawn over them, and generally bend over backwards to do everything in their power to win over the porcupine. They work so hard for so long that sometimes they actually succeed! But at what cost?

You may win the battle, but you'll absolutely lose the war. Audiences aren't stupid. Not only do they know when someone's inappropriate, they know when the presenter is working a little too hard to get on his or her good side. The audience not only perceives this as a reflection of weakness, they see a presenter actually rewarding bad behavior.

By the way, other than watching the rhythm of a program completely throw off by wasting a ton of time trying to placate the porcupine, how many times have you actually witnessed a presenter truly successfully turn around a porcupine's ridiculous behavior by simply being nice?

The solution is easier than you than you think, but harder than you might imagine; leave the porcupine alone. Remember, no matter how long you there is no quota system for participation. When it's time to ask him or her a question, make it a fact-based question so there's little wiggle room for pontification. When it's time for a small group activity, you assign the leaders and spokespeople for each group. Hold questions from the audience to the end of each segment, and don't be afraid to take a porcupine's question offline if it's inappropriate. It's your program, and your rules; don't be afraid to tighten those rules for the sake of the rest of the audience.

The fact is you just can't hug a porcupine. If you try to, you'll feel the pain of a porcupine who is well vested in his or her behavior and doesn't want to be hugged, and an audience who will lose respect for you if you do. I'd suggest you trust your instincts if you actually *did* see a porcupine walk into your program. Leave it alone!

What if I could provide you with two special words; These two words are so powerful that they can help you in almost any professional interaction you might find yourself in. I'll tell you what these two words are when you read…

The Great Equalizers

For years, I've specialized in two different topics: I teach people how to influence the actions of others one-on-one, and I teach people how to influence the actions of others through presentations to groups of people.

I have modules that teach how to initiate a conversation, create trust, lay out techniques to create urgency, closing techniques, sustaining interest ideas, negotiation tactics, and in the words of Al Pacino, "I'm just gettin' warmed up!" Despite all the tactics and techniques I teach, the most important thing that I can share with my students is to remember two words that I call, "the great equalizers." I call them, "the great equalizers" because remembering these two words can offset just about any jam you can get yourself into.

I recently chose these two words to apply to a giveaway I've prepared. I decided to create my own Bobble-Head, called a "Robble-Head," to be precise, to give away in seminars. When the company that makes them asked me what words I wanted on the base, I thought long and hard. What words would transcend any message or topic, and would be appropriate for all audiences? Then it came to me: I must put the two words that represent "the great equalizer" on the base. What are the two words I've been teasing you with? The words are "Energy & Enthusiasm!"

Losing sleep over an interview? Worried about a big presentation you have to deliver? Anxious about a sales call you're about to make? Meeting a new person you really want to click with? No matter what  the worry might be, if you remember these two words, and adhere to their meaning, you'll be just fine.

The fact is... the world will not come to an end if you do not follow all the lessons I teach, or if you forget to create trust, or urgency, or if you don't apply appropriate closing techniques. People will naturally forgive just about anything. Forget to ask questions? Clients will frequently provide you with information anyway. Apply incorrect closing techniques? Clients will frequently commit anyway. Lose a visual, forget a handout, or fail to establish utilities in a presentation you might be delivering? People will forgive you. In fact, people will forgive just about anything, but they won't forgive a lack of energy and enthusiasm.

In case you're wondering how seriously I take these two words, I've been wearing a silver lightning bolt on the lapel of my suit jacket, sports coat, or collar of my shirt without fail. It's a quiet ritual I go through to pause and take a moment to remember just how important this lesson is. Oh, and I've been doing this ritual for over 40 years.

The next time you find your pulse racing over an impending anxious situation; don't focus on the variables you cannot control. Instead, focus on what you can control. You can *always* control your energy & enthusiasm, "the great equalizers." Now I have a "Robble-Head" that will help you remember that!

If the thought of sweating makes you squeamish, you might want to a pass on this particular Blarticle®. I'm not just going to talk about it; I'm going to celebrate it! Sweat is one of the best measurements afforded any presenter. I'll tell you more about it when you read…

Let Them See You Sweat!

Sweat. Just the thought of it bothers some people. At my health club, the place is littered with towels – made available just to capture your sweat. Most of us want to challenge ourselves when we work out, so we try to consistently wipe away our own sweat so we won't offend others who are nearby.

Personally, I've never really had an issue with sweat. As a matter of fact, I kind of like it. Sweat encourages me. Sweat motivates me. Sweat provides a report card on just how intense my workout is, and how much effort I'm putting into it. When I walk by others who are working out, I can usually tell their level of effort by the amount of sweat I see. When you walk by someone who is moving slowly on their bike or elliptical, often reading a magazine or talking on a phone, you won't see a lot of sweat.

Even though I may sweat when I work out, my favorite time to sweat is when I'm giving a presentation. The mere act of sweating inspires me, and when I see it from another speaker, it impresses me. It says, "Look out folks; I am dialed in and I'm giving you every bit of energy I have in the tank! I am *right here – right now! This very moment* is all that matters to me!"

Believe it or not, it takes a lot of effort for a presenter to actually sweat. That sweat isn't coming from anxiety, or from running, or from lifting heavy objects. Usually, the temperature in the room is on the cooler side to make the audience comfortable, so you can't say the presenter is sweating due to the heat.

So what's making the presenter sweat? Pure, unadulterated effort and intensity! You won't ever see that level of intensity from those who tuck themselves comfortably behind a lectern. You'll see it from those who are fighting for far more than that. When every word is punched, every sentence has meaning, every gesture has a purpose, and every step is a lunge, you'll see sweat!

So, when you give your next presentation, I want you to sweat. It's going to take a level of intensity you might not be accustomed to, but if you want it badly enough, I'm sure you can do it. And when you feel that sweat dripping down your face, and off your ears, nose, and chin do me a small favor; don't touch it. Don't wipe it away. Let your audience get a good look at it. Enjoy it and celebrate the effort you are putting forth. Let them see you sweat!

This past week, I witnessed a classic mistake made by presenters. I'll not only tell you what it is, but I'll also tell you how to make sure it doesn't happen to you when you read...

It's All in the Timing

It happened again. I see it all the time. I watched as a professional speaker fell prey to the same mistake amateurs make all the time. I'm referring to losing your timing in a presentation.

We've all seen the telltale signs. We sit through fifty minutes of a one-hour presentation that seems to meander a bit, and then suddenly the speaker puts the throttle down for those final few minutes. As we watch the slides being shown, we hear clever lines like this: "We won't be needing to cover that," or "That's not as important to get to." Well, if it wasn't important, why is it in the handout that you passed out to the audience? It's a mistake that has plagued speakers forever. Let's take a look at the two major issues that usually cause this problem.

1. Uncertainty. Unless you are a professional speaker who delivers one particular presentation frequently, timing is almost always an uncertainty. Even though you may have practiced in an empty room or in front of a mirror, that does not come close to simulating the give and take that goes on in a live presentation. When in doubt, speakers will *always* put in too much information to avoid the dreaded "running out of material" nightmare.
2. Unknowns. Sometimes audience members ask questions. Sometimes the audience takes longer than expected to finish an exercise. Sometimes a speaker finds an inspirational

moment in his or her delivery, and loses track of time. All of these unknowns contribute to timing issues.

Now, let's look at the solutions:

1. Break it up. No matter what the length the presentation might be, create a one-page agenda that you can keep an eye on, and break the timing of that agenda up into four equal parts. If your presentation is an hour long, break it into 15-minute segments. If it's three hours, break it into 45-minute segments.
2. Think of a hot air balloon. When I deliver a presentation, I always visualize the timing of my presentation like flying in a hot air balloon. Let's say my goal is to keep that balloon 2,000 feet in the air. When that balloon goes to 2,200 feet, I cool it down, and the balloon comes down slowly. When that balloon goes to 1,800 feet, I add a little heat and bring it back up. Now see your presentation as you see that balloon. When you hit that first quarter mark in your presentation, check your timing. Is that presentation running too quickly? Ask the audience some questions. Break into a story or two you keep in reserve. Edge off the throttle, and ease that balloon back down a few hundred feet. When you hit the next quarter check your timing. Is that presentation running too slowly? Leave out that unnecessary story you tell from time to time. Shorten your delivery a bit. For those audience members with their hands up, tell them this: "Let me take one last question, and please hold the rest until we reach the end of this presentation. Then I'll be sure to answer every question you might have." Lightly hit that throttle, and ease that balloon back up a few hundred feet.

The key is this: Don't wait until the presentation is 90% complete to begin to gauge that balloon. When you lose your timing, that frenetic finish is all the audience is left with. However, when you complete a presentation without rushing, or slowing down it's a thing of beauty. It's like jumping off a balance beam and sticking your landing without a hop. Ease the timing of that presentation up or down throughout the delivery, and you won't find yourself jolting that audience back to earth when the presentation comes in for a landing. You'll know you stuck that landing because those who brought you there, the audience will be applauding and appreciative of your timing.

F or years I taught every trainer at Xerox how to give presentations, have given countless presentations of my own for decades, and have written a Bestselling book on the topic. That doesn't mean I'm not susceptible to making costly mistakes of my own. I'll tell you a doozy of a mistake I made, and one I want you to avoid when you read…

Not Leaving Well Enough Alone

As a student of the presentation game, I've watched a lot of presentations in my life. After a while, you can quickly get a sense of those that know what they're doing, and those that struggle a bit. Unfortunately, recently I joined the ranks of the "struggle a bit" crowd, and if it can happen to me, it can certainly happen to you. The problem? Not leaving well enough alone.

It started harmlessly enough; I was creating a presentation for a charity event. I put just enough creative touches into the presentation to make it interesting, without taking away from the presentation itself. Then I did something I don't recommend others do: I kept picking at it.

It began with a few extra sound effects. After all, putting a couple of sound effects into a presentation isn't exactly going to ruin the presentation! Besides, it made me laugh, and if it made me laugh, I knew it was going to make my audience laugh.

Then I began to insert small bits within the presentation, designed to involve the audience. I had a couple strategically placed, and I thought they would create magical moments. Since they looked so good, I put in more – a lot more. I figured they would just strengthen the presentation.

Finally, the flood gates opened and I incorporated video, I inserted multiple presentation fonts, templates, transitions, and other presentation gimmicks. (I mean special effects.) I even found a 20-foot ladder, which I covered with fabric and strategically placed so I could dramatically climb it and continue my presentation towering above my audience. Yes, I was going to take this audience to a place they had never been to before! I had a fever, and that fever was called, "More-Is-Better-Itus."

Why do so many of us believe that the more we put into a presentation, the better the presentation will be? Are we using the sound, video, templates, transitions, fonts, and gimmicks to build a better presentation? Or could we just be using them as a crutch? It's a strange irony because the more *stuff* we put into a presentation, the weaker the presentation becomes. The reason for this is simple: The *stuff* ultimately gets in the way of the actual content.

That's exactly what occurred in the presentation I delivered recently. I was consumed by a bad case of "More-Is-Better-Itus." I threw everything but the kitchen sink at an audience, and my reward was a confused, detached audience that seemed frequently distracted and unable to focus on the content of the presentation. Someone was distracting them, and that someone was me.

The next time you have a presentation that looks sharp and ready to go, please heed my advice: Don't listen to that voice in your head that wants to keep adding more. You may be getting a little bored with this presentation as you're practicing it over and over, but that audience you are going to address has never heard it before! Leave the *stuff* out, and remember these wise words… Leave Well Enough Alone!

Conducting seminars in Switzerland gave me the privilege of visiting a beautiful country, and working with extraordinary people. It also provided me with a reminder of an old lesson I learned about motivation. I'll tell you what that lesson was when you read...

A Reason to Try

You'd think that, after thirty years of delivering seminars all over the world, it would get old and less exciting for me. Oh, some deliveries are easier than others, but last week was special. Last week's seminar provided me with plenty of motivation to do my best because I found myself in one of the most beautiful cities in the world: I was in Bern,
Switzerland. Once there, I quickly realized that the beauty of the city was exceeded only by the kindness of the people who reside there. What a week it was, and personally, I believe the fine folks got one heck of a show from Rob Jolles. After all, I had a reason to try.

Being invited to travel so far to do your job provides tremendous motivation to try your hardest. I had nine hours in a plane to think about how important this delivery was. I had time to think about the added travel expenses involved in bringing me to Switzerland. I had time to think about the faith my client had placed in me by seeking me out after reading my book, and wanting to implement my ideas within their organization. I even had time to think about my personal pride of being an American citizen, and I wanted to represent my country in the proper way.

You would think that I had plenty to worry about in those nine hours, but the opposite was true. I had a reason to try to do my very best, and I was grateful to have this added motivation in my mind. As a matter of fact, I'm always grateful to have a reason to try.

Occasionally, I've had clients who have said comments like this: "I don't want to make you anxious, but the head of distribution will be attending your session," or "I hope I'm not making you nervous, but so much is riding on your delivery." Nervous?! One would think so, but I am actually happy when clients share that kind of information with me. It gives me a reason to try. My concern is when I *don't* have a reason to try.

Well, I sure had a reason to try last week, and with that reason to try, I gave that client every bit of energy I had. I think the sessions I delivered exceeded everyone's expectations. I even had another nine hours flying home to think about it. What I thought about was this; what happens when you *can't* find a reason to try?

What happens when there is no head of distribution in the room, or there isn't a lot riding on your delivery, or you aren't traveling to some exotic land, or you aren't carrying the personal pride of your nation, or you've done a job for so long you can't find a reason to try?

Somewhere over the Atlantic Ocean, I figured out the answer to this important question. We *always* have a reason to try because the greatest motivator is our personal pride to do our best. That pride exists within all of us, and it shouldn't need prompting from other people or situations. At the end of the day, it comes down to how we sign our work. We are the only ones who truly know how much effort we put into something. We just need to remember to dig deep, and look for that energy and enthusiasm inside each of us. Our reason to try really needs no prompting from others because it comes from within.

Personal Growth

This section of the book focuses on personal growth and explores the mindset shifts and habits that lead to resilience, adaptability, and success. It will challenge you to overcome self-imposed limitations, and unexpected wisdom found in everyday moments. From taking risks to refining communication and learning from failure, this section will encourage you to step outside your comfort zones and grow into your full potential.

How many times have you heard someone say, "I don't want to get my hopes up!" Really? Well, I hope I can change your point of view, when you read…

Is There a Penalty for Hope?

Let me start by saying this: I think we underestimate hope. Hope gets us through tough times. Although sometimes we may choose to give up on hope, hope will never desert us. Hope doesn't hold grudges. Hope is only a thought away, and a powerful ally. Hope sounds like the perfect companion, but if that's so, how come we are so quick to give up on hope?

When I hear people say, "I don't want to get my hopes up," it makes me wince. Why the heck would you be afraid to get your hopes up?

When was the last time your effort was reduced as a result of getting your hopes up? I've never seen or heard of anyone who failed because they hoped too hard. In fact, the opposite is true. When you have hope, and I mean *real* hope, the chance of succeeding doesn't get reduced. It's simply not possible. Hope provides energy. It provides resolve. It provides strength. It provides confidence. Hope can inspire you to do great things. So why are so many of us afraid to embrace hope, particularly when we seem to need it the most? What are we so fearful of?

It turns out there is a penalty for hope. That penalty is disappointment. When you get your hopes up and fail, disappointment is sure to follow. When this happens, we frequently lash out at hope. We tend to blame our failure on the fact that we hoped for something too much. Rather than blaming ourselves for our failures, we curse the concept of hope by saying, "if only I hadn't gotten my hopes up!"

Do you know what's worse than the sting of disappointment? The regret that comes with being too afraid to hope, because that particular fear is frequently followed by being too afraid to try… and that just can't happen. *Maybe* you could have been successful, but you were too afraid of getting your hopes up, so you didn't try.

Avoiding hope in order to avoid disappointment just doesn't make sense, and I hope you agree with that. I say this: Throw caution to the wind, and the next time you are pursuing something that isn't 100% under your control, give yourself a double dose of hope. I hope you'll succeed, but if you don't, try not to blame your disappointment on too much hope. Instead, graciously accept the minor penalty of disappointment that goes hand in hand with having high hopes. Just try to learn from the experience, and get ready to hope some more!

Sometimes what some people call "bad luck," other people call "good fortune." What if I told you that having a positive outlook would not only reduce your stress, it would improve your luck? Well, it can, and I'll prove it to you when you read…

Sometimes what some people call "bad luck," other people call "good fortune." What if I told you that having a positive outlook would not only reduce your stress, it would improve your luck? Well, it can, and I'll prove it to you when you read...

A Tale of Two Stories

Story #1...

Last week, the travel Gods really stuck it to me good. I showed up at O'Hare airport at 6:00 pm, and I found out that my 7:00 pm flight back to National Airport was running thirty minutes late. This was due to thunderstorm activity. When I noticed that there was a flight to Dulles Airport that was also delayed but set to leave at 6:30 pm, I made a run for the gate. The 6:30 pm departure was an airline fairy-tale because the plane wasn't even in yet. What's more, I had to wait in a 45-minute line just to see if I could get on the plane that wasn't even here yet. While waiting, my original 7:30 pm flight was cancelled, and my rare United first-class upgrade was lost as well. I ended up getting on the "6:30pm flight," which left the gate two hours late, sat on the tarmac for another hour and a half, and didn't get me back to Dulles until midnight.

What a lousy night. I couldn't catch a break.

Story #2...

Last week, the travel Gods were really looking out for me. I showed up at O'Hare airport at 6:00 pm and I found out that my 7:00 pm flight back to National Airport was running thirty minutes late. This was due to thunderstorm activity. With many flights cancelling, I felt pretty lucky to even have a flight that wasn't cancelled, but I figured a smart use of my time would be to check out a flight to Dulles that was running an hour ahead of my flight. I made it to this other gate and although the line was long, I had a good book. I felt that I was being prudent by waiting to see if I could get on standby on this flight, rather than just sitting and doing nothing. I got lucky because my 7:30 pm flight ended up cancelling, and the line I was in grew longer, and longer. We loaded late, and a thunderstorm hit right after we had boarded the plane, so we had to wait out on the tarmac for a while. At least we were all on board! We were also going to be in line to take off as soon as the skies cleared. It cost us a few hours, but when they opened back up, we were ready to roll. There was a lot of traffic on that tarmac, adding another 90 minutes or so, but with so many flights cancelled, I was thrilled to be one of the lucky ones to make it home that night.

It was a good night because I caught not one, but two breaks. The first break I caught was when I decided to wait in that line around 6:00 pm, a full hour before my flight cancelled. The second break I caught was my ticket. United had moved me up to first-class on my original flight so I was holding a first-class ticket. Although they didn't a first-class seat available, that little gem of an upgrade moved me to the top of the standby list. I felt so lucky to have been given a seat on one of the few planes to make it back to D.C.!

You've just read about one, true event, told in two dramatically different ways. Now, I'll bet you're wondering where the concept of luck comes into this particular event. The truth is, luck *does* play a part in all of this. You'll notice in story #2, there are several moments in the story that deal with the positive side of the problem at hand. Research has shown that lucky people usually see the positive side of their bad luck. I'm sure you'll agree that our attitude plays a part in the luck we often enjoy.

In story #2, you'll also notice moments in the story when I observed how much more difficult the situation was for others. Once again,

NOT A BLOG ~ NOT AN ARTICLE ~ A BLARTICLE®

research has shown that lucky people tend to look at their bad luck and imagine how things could have been worse. Certainly, you'll agree that it helps if you can remove the cloud of bad luck, and perceive the same situation with perspective.

Our attitude and perception can work for us or against us. Every life has its share of positive and negative moments. If we feel downtrodden and unlucky during those moments that challenge us, how in the world can that contribute to a positive attitude? Not only that, we might not be open to the opportunities that we can take to help alleviate the situation if we're bogged down with negativity. When we take those challenging moments, and truly believe in a different story, we put ourselves in a position to maintain a positive state of mind. No matter what the obstacle is, we might actually gain something from the experience at hand. So, the question really is, how will you tell your story[1]?

---

1. The750-word… usually rule was broken here, but in fairness, I did tell two stories!

Not many of us get a second chance to rewrite a tough moment from our past. But this week, I found myself standing in front of an audience in Los Angeles with a rare opportunity—a business 'do-over.' But first I had to quiet a voice that was bound and determined to undermine my success. It's a voice that you hear too now and then, and I'll tell you about it when you read…

Taming the Victim Voice

This week I found myself out in Los Angeles with a rare opportunity. I had the opportunity to perform a business "do-over." Let me jump in the "Way Back Machine" and give you the back-story here.

Six years ago, I conducted a seminar in Las Vegas that did not go well. That didn't just bother me, it became an obsession. That's because when you give seminars for a living it is not only unacceptable to put on a bad seminar, it can be damaging to your career. In 25 years of delivering seminars this may have been the second seminar that was not appreciated by a client. What's more, I felt the problems within the seminar were not only not my fault, the feedback was unfair.

It was unfair because rather than a training room, my client had me conduct the seminar in a hotel room. Rather than a screen for an LCD projector to show my PowerPoint presentation, I was asked to project on a wall where a hotel picture once had been. Rather than a room full of eager participants, I was presented with about ten distracted individuals. It wasn't their fault; this can happen when the environment is wrong, and you are delivering a seminar in someone's hotel room.

If you feel sorry for me, don't be. I'm not telling you that I didn't feel sorry for myself at the time, but that was the "Victim Voice" in me making some noise. The "Victim Voice" in me wanted to keep reminding me how unfair everything was, and how nothing was my fault. I'll be you have that voice speaking to you from time to time as well. Don't listen to it. If you do, your reward will be to make the same mistakes again... over and over again. That comes with the territory when nothing is ever your fault.

I told you what was unfair, but I forgot to remind you that, much like the world you come from, often things are unfair. Our choice is to do the best we can we've the hand we have to play, or we can blame someone else. It's easy to pick the latter, but I'll pick door number one. I could have kept the laptop in the bag, and not used my precious PowerPoint. I could have put in a few more small group exercises when I saw the group was going to be a challenging one. I could have battled that audience's apathy with more energy from me. And I could have reconfigured that room to be more conducive to learning. Instead, I initially blamed everything and everyone but me.

Thankfully, I only listened to that annoying "Victim Voice" for a short period of time. I then woke up, took responsibility, and vowed to my client it would never happen again. Rather than become defensive with my client, I took responsibility. A few weeks ago that client asked me to speak again. This blog is not intended to be a blog about how great Rob Jolles is, but I will tell you that today's session was a whole lot better than the last one. Some would say I was lucky. I'd prefer to say I applied what I learned from the mistakes I made, and put those lessons to good use not just for this audience, but for many audiences I have worked with since that fateful delivery in Las Vegas.

Want to know if your "Victim Voice" is overpowering you? Ask yourself this question every time you feel something unfair has happened to you. "If I could do this again, what would I do differently?" If the answer is, "nothing", you are a victim. If the answer is anything besides "nothing", you are on your way to not only defeating that "Victim Voice", but learning from it and acquiring wisdom.

As for me, I'm smiling broadly as I write this. If doing poorly years ago for this client didn't bother me, I would be disappointed in myself. However, I didn't just learn from it. Today, I got another shot at making things right, and I didn't waste that opportunity. I wonder if I would have even been given this opportunity yet alone been successful with it if I had let that "Victim Voice" have its way.

There's nothing like getting on a roll and enjoying the temporary invincibility success brings. Wouldn't you like to bottle that up and somehow tap into it when things aren't going so well? Well, I believe there is a technique that can do just that, and I'll tell you what it is when you read…

What Would You Attempt to Do…

The mind is an amazing mechanism, but it sure can fool you. Left unchecked, it can convince you of all sorts of things. When the body is injured, the mind can convince you you're just fine. When you hear something that goes bump in the night, the mind can convince you that there's trouble where there isn't any. And when our spirit is low,  sometimes the mind can convince you that this is where our spirit belongs.

Think about it for a moment. Surely there have been times in your life when everything you touched seemed to work out for the best. During those times, you sailed along without a care in the world. The mind was there for the ride, and it did its part too. The mind gave you hope and optimism, and you believed that whatever came next was going to follow the same pattern of success.

Of course, no life is without defeat, and sometimes those defeats bring about pain and worry. The mind is part of that too, and hope and optimism are replaced with doubt and pessimism. Worst of all, the mind convinces you to no longer believe in yourself.

Who says the mind is always right? Do we really have to wait around until life presents us with a string of successes to convince our minds to let us believe in ourselves once again? We are far more believable to others when we believe in ourselves. So who says we can't *fool* the mind to believe?

Watch a method actor perform and you'll see what I mean by fooling the mind. Method acting is a group of techniques that actors use to create in themselves the thoughts and feelings of their characters. The result is that they can develop lifelike performances. For example, when an actor cries on stage and produces real tears, often those tears are not coming from the lines that are being recited. The tears are coming from that actor's ability to take his or her mind to another moment when the tears were real.

Much like that actor, when we are struggling to believe in ourselves, we too can take our mind to another moment in time when we *did* believe. Whether it's selling a new client, selling a prospective employer, or perhaps just selling ourselves, I can guarantee you that taking your mind to a place of accomplishment can only increase your chances of success.

I'd like to introduce you to a quote by Robert Schuller; I keep this in my office and I have it in a visible place so I can glance at it from time to time. It's a quote my son wears on a chain around his neck and it's a quote I'd like share with you:

"What would you attempt to do if you knew you could not fail?"

So often we become obsessed with the words we choose thinking these words will get others to believe us. If you take yourself to a place you've been when you *knew* you could not fail, the words will follow… but that's not all. Your mind will be more than happy to surround those words with a more credible and positive vocal pitch, pace, tone, facial expressions, and other nonverbal behaviors. When you behave in that way, it can ignite a passion and a confidence that will be clearly visible to others.

It gives me goose bumps to think of the victories that will follow.

It's early in the morning, and the alarm goes off. It doesn't matter if it buzzes, bings, plays music or rings, it's never a welcome sound. But what comes next fascinates me because I think it provides a quick glimpse into our personalities. I'll tell you all about it when you read…

You Snooze, You Lose

They say opposites attract, and each morning, it's on display in my house when the alarm goes off. My wife, Ronni, loves the snooze bar. She seems to look forward to not just tapping it or hitting it; when she goes for the snooze bar, she smacks it! It's almost a part of her waking up ritual. If she wants to get up at 7:30 am, she sets her alarm for 6:45 am so she can smack that snooze bar around for the next 45 minutes.

I'm just not a snooze bar guy. Quite frankly, I don't even like the name "snooze bar." I think it should be renamed, "lazy bar." I can tell you right now, without hesitation, I have never hit, the snooze bar over the past 40 years. I don't know where to find it, how it works, or how much time it gives you to *not* wake up. The fact is this: I don't believe in snooze bars.

Now, this doesn't make me right or others wrong… exactly. I'm sure there are plenty of good reasons to hit the snooze bar. Maybe you accidentally set the clock ten minutes earlier than you meant to. Maybe you forgot this was your morning to sleep ten minutes later than usual. Maybe you wanted to wake your spouse up, and then get yourself up ten minutes later to keep from bumping into each other in the bathroom.

I'm guessing there are plenty of people in this world who are fully functioning members of society and probably don't take too kindly to my over opinionated attack on the lowly snooze bar... wherever it's located! But in defense of those who just can't hit that, uh, thing, let me tell you why we can't do it. It's because we're afraid.

We're afraid that somehow, the act of hitting that bar will spill into other aspects of our lives. After all, who actually hears the sound of the alarm going off and really *wants* to get out of bed?! That goes for brushing our teeth, showering, shaving, getting to work on time, and so much more. It's not easy, but day after day, we do these things because we know that's what we have to do to ultimately improve our chances of success.

Imagine if there was some weird bar that we could keep hitting to put off everything we didn't want to do. You don't really have to imagine too hard because they exist and are all around us.

- When we don't want to get to concentrate and get down to work, we hit the snooze bar and play one more game of solitaire.
- When we don't want to make a difficult call, or finish a difficult assignment, we hit the snooze bar and answer a few meaningless emails that could clearly wait.
- When we don't want to complete an overdue project around the house, we hit the snooze bar and work on just about anything meaningless we can get our hands on.

I'm quite sure there are many who can competently manage the lazy... I mean, the snooze bar, and keep it from infecting their lives. The truth is, I'm just not one of them. As one of my favorite comedians, (other than my son), Jim Gaffigan once said of the snooze bar, "Nothing like starting off the day with a little procrastination. As my first decision of the day... I will go back to sleep." Nope; I don't want to know where it's located, nor will I ever hit it. For those who do: vive la différence!

It seems strange to think that the natural strengths we possess can somehow get in the way of our success. But they can, and I'll tell you how that can happen and what you can do about it when you read…

Going to Your Off-Hand

I have always enjoyed the game of basketball. Not blessed with great height, I fell in love with the position of point guard. The position allowed me to relay plays being sent in by my coaches, and manage the flow of the game. It was the perfect position for a smaller player who liked to lead and control things.

Being left-handed gave me an initial advantage over my opponents. Since most defenders assumed I was right-handed and I would most likely be moving to my right, I had the element of surprise. It's not unusual for coaches and players to study their opponents during warm-ups. Knowing this, I developed my own, sneaky way of warming up. Although I was uncomfortable dribbling or moving to my right, I'd warm-up almost exclusively using my right hand. Then, once the game began, I would dribble the ball up court with my right hand, and as soon as I got near the top of the key, cross over to my left. This always left my defender flatfooted. From there, I would drive to the basket for an easy lay-up. This little trick never failed to work… the first time. With my defender thinking it was an anomaly, it would often work the second time too.

But by the third time, my defender would be waiting for me. The element of surprise had been replaced by predictability. Going to my left was easy and natural to me, but I knew what I had to do in order to become a much better player. I had to put in the time and effort to learn how to use my other hand, or what basketball players call the "off-hand."

In baseball, this off-hand is the difference between learning to hit a fastball, and learning to hit a curveball. In tennis, it's the difference between learning to hit a flat serve and a kick serve. In golf, it's the difference between learning to hit a golf ball, and learning t spin a golf ball.

Sound familiar? In business, we often operate in one of two areas. One area is that place where everything feels natural and effortless. These are the areas that makes us feel confident, and where we are often celebrated by others for our expertise and accomplishments. These are the areas that make us good at what we do.

The other area is the area that represents our off-hand. It's the part of our job that does not feel natural or effortless. We don't feel confident and we try hard to avoid using these off-hand skills. When we avoid what doesn't come naturally, we find that the off-hand becomes weaker and weaker. What's more, to avoid using our off-hand we begin to make it obvious to others just what our strengths and weaknesses are. You would think that seeing someone excel at a particular skill would put him or her in a position of strength, but I feel it does the complete opposite. The truth is that it makes us one dimensional and vulnerable. Vulnerable to what you might ask? Change.

When actors are celebrated for incredible, focused portrayals of a certain type of character, they are assigned a word that makes them shutter. The word is "typecast." If there's a role to be played that matches directly with their celebrated strength, they're hired. But track the life of so many of your favorite actors who were typecast in specific roles. Things changed, and the very strength that brought them to the pinnacle of success eventually became their downfall. The smart ones took roles early to play against their stereotypes, and they survived. The others never developed their "off-hand" characters and they faded into obscurity.

If you want to be good at anything, by all means continue to shine in the light your natural and celebrated skills. But Voltaire once said, "Good is the enemy of great." If you want to be great, identify that off-hand and work twice as hard to develop it. If writing is a weakness, enroll in an adult education program. If you find you avoid public speaking at all costs, join Toastmasters. If selling is something you hate to do, read one of my books and give me a call! While you're improving that "off hand," be prepared to be frustrated, and you will have to fight off the voices in your head that will tempt you to return to your more natural ways. Continue to work hard and a whole new level of success awaits.

Have you ever driven down the road on a cold and rainy Sunday, and seen a miserable looking runner? I'll bet you thought this: "Why in the world would that person pick a day like today to run?" Well, I've been that runner, and there's a lot more to that picture than you might imagine. I'll tell you what it is, and why you might think twice about what you are seeing when you read…

The Schmuck Running in the Rain

When I was younger, I used to love to run. I started by running 10-kilometer races, and then I graduated to 10-milers, moved on to half marathons, and before I knew it, I was running marathons. People would ask me: "What's it like training for a marathon?" I'd always have the same answer: "You have to be willing to do some running in the rain." I'd smile to myself because I knew most people had no idea what I was talking about. For me, "running in the rain" has always been a metaphor for something much greater.

A race of 26.2 miles is not something to be taken lightly. Most people on this earth cannot just show up and run a marathon, and yet, almost anyone can complete one. How can that be? You just need to have a commitment to train properly. That commitment involves your nutrition and setting goals for yourself. The most important part of the puzzle, however, is the dedication to run a certain number of miles each week.

For me, I made a commitment to run 35 miles every week. I typically liked to break those miles up into five different runs, and each run was a certain distance. No matter how many runs I planned or how long each one was, the weekly mileage total was nonnegotiable. Depending on my travel schedule, family obligations, weather, and personal mood, some weeks were easier than others, but I *never* missed getting my 35 miles a week in.

Notice I put an emphasis on the word, *"never."* That's because I have always been suspicious and untrusting of the word, "usually." There are too many things that can affect something we "usually" do. I could fall prey to the voices in my head that were masterful at providing a litany of excuses as to why I didn't have to run that day, or that week. There could always be extenuating circumstances, which really meant that I just couldn't fulfill my 35 miles that week. It's amazing how much louder those voices get once that first commitment is broken.

Now, I don't mean that I didn't have my fair share of Sundays with a mileage count that was behind where it should have been, and some of those Sundays were pretty rainy, but out I went. I had no one to blame but myself. I was the shmuck you saw running in the rain.

That philosophy has served me well in business, and in life. When I wrote my first book in 1993, I didn't have a mentor and I knew little about how to tackle a project like that. What I did know was this: To me, it represented a marathon of sorts, and I treated it as such. Instead of a weekly mileage count, I created a weekly page count. I heard the same voices in my head that whisper: "It's just not your week; you'll get 'em next week for sure!" Only now, those voices are only whispers because they know I won't listen.

It has also served many others I mentor – including a good friend of mine who is writing a book. He has never let his busy and challenging life get in the way of achieving the page count he committed to. He still has some unpleasant "Sunday nights," when he is doing his own kind of run in the rain: He has to stay up very late to write those pages he promised himself he would. He's not sad, and he's not to be pitied. He's just making good on the commitment he made. He's also on his way to becoming a published author, and it is mostly because he has allowed nothing to get in the way of the writing of his weekly number of pages.

Not a Blog ~ Not an Article ~ A Blarticle®

You don't have to be training for a marathon, or writing a book, to connect with this message. We all set goals; some are immediate, and some are long-term. It's those long-term goals that require those short-term commitments. Sometimes we may hit some cold and rainy Sunday nights, but we still have to lace up those shoes and run.

The next time you pass by a shmuck running in the rain, perhaps you'll see someone else. If you take a real close look as you go by, you may see what I see; someone with a sense of pride along with a wry smile that says, "next week, I'm going to run in the sun!"

This week I'm going to tell you a true story about two people. It's a story that plays out in so many lives when these two personalities collide, and the results are disturbing. But there *is* a lesson to be learned for every one of us, and you'll see what I mean when you read...

The Pig Farmer and the Intellectual

There once was a woman who grew up on a farm in South Dakota. Her family raised pigs. She worked hard, and the farm was successful, but she longed for something better in her life. So, she left the farm, went to school, graduated, and moved to the big city. There she found a job, worked hard, and became a manager. She wasn't the smartest, or  the most popular, or the easiest person to get along with, but what she carved out a place for herself, and was a competent employee.

At the same time, there once was a woman who grew up in the big city. She was very bright. She worked hard too, and was very competent wherever she worked. She wasn't always the most popular, but her focus was on getting the job right, and that she did.

One day the intellectual was hired to work for the pig farmer. They came from different worlds, and saw things in different ways. The pig farmer was fiercely proud of her accomplishments, and her position within the company, and saw the intellectual as a threat. Soon they because involved in a project, a marketing study. The pig farmer felt it would be a waste of time and less than 200 people would take the survey. They began to fight over how to complete the project each claiming their way was the better way. The pig farmer stood her ground as did the intellectual. The intellectual was sure the marketing study would be successful and after pleading her case to the CEO who hired her, put out the survey.

It turned out the intellectual was right when a staggering 3,200 people took the survey. In fact, the survey provided an enormous amount of valuable data. Later that day the CEO, who hired her called her on the phone and said, "This is your last day here. You've obviously proven incapable of working with your colleague to get your work done. It isn't working, and it isn't going to work so I need you to pack up and someone will escort you out."

Was the intellectual right? Yes. Was the treatment of the intellectual unfair? Sure. Now what?

This is not an uncommon scenario, in fact, it's far too common particularly with those who I will loosely categorize as "intellectuals." This is a society that I clearly do not belong to, but I've certainly seen my share of in my day. Sadly, although the names change, the basic script remains the same including the part about the intellectuals far too often getting a phone call, and being escorted out of the building.

In school being right seems to trump all other reason. In business, and in life, almost the opposite is true. The companies I worked for prioritized being a team player, getting along with others, and getting along with your manager far above being the smartest person on the team. Quite simply, here's what I believe to be true:

- It's *not* always about being right. It's about being a team player.
- It's *okay* to be the smartest person in the room, but at the right time, and in the right way.
- It's *not* okay making others around you feel less intelligent than you… ever.

Not a Blog ~ Not an Article ~ A Blarticle®

There's a time, a place, and a way to be right. It's a blind spot, not just for intellectuals but for anyone who places being right above being sensitive to your surroundings. Allowing others to be right, even when you believe there is a better way, is not a weakness of character; it displays a strength in character. It's not about being right; it's about *when* to be right.

The other day, I met with an individual who reminded me of myself twenty years ago, and it startled me. He relished in the belief that no matter what the consequences, you must never back down when you know you are right. It made me sad, and I'll tell you why when you read...

The Cost of Being Right

One of the benefits of being raised by a marine was that I was taught the meaning of courage. My father was a corpsman in not one, but two, wars, and the courage he displayed was beyond imagination. At an early age, my father demanded that I learn how to be courageous. I was willing to do anything to win my father's favor, so I eagerly complied. This

trait was instilled in me, and it is something I'm fiercely proud of. It has served me well... most of the time.

When I was pushed, I pushed back; when I was shouted at, I shouted back; and when I had the right answer, I fought like heck to be heard. But each push, shout, and fight came at a cost. The most severe of which was the cost of being right.

It's amazing how many business schools miss this simple message. As a business major at the University of Maryland, I learned the principles of business, economics, accounting, statistics, and so much more. One thing I was never taught was about the real-world politics of business. Without a teacher, I was left to my own instincts, and the instincts of my father. Those instincts served him well in the marines. They also served him well in his career as a salesman. He was a damn good salesman, but he never really had to deal with corporate politics. When you work for an organization that is driven by sales, and you outsell those around you as he did, there are no politics.

I had no use for company politics, and took pride in being known as a guy who would never be silent when he knew he was right. I welcomed the price for being right because I knew the courage it took to do so. I battled management when I knew I was right, and I battled my coworkers when I knew I was right. I might even dare to admit that a part of me, deep down inside, enjoyed it. One of my favorite sayings was this: When I'm no longer on this earth, they are going to put on my tombstone: "This man never backed down when he knew he was right!" I wore my beliefs like a badge, and I carried that mantra with an enormous level of satisfaction. I was wrong.

I felt that others viewed me as a courageous person, and I thought I was respected because I had the nerve to say what I believed. Looking back now, I'm quite sure many did not view me in that way. I believe I was viewed as a person who did not fit into the machinery of the corporation, and therefore, I was an obstruction to the organization. The corporation put up with me because I worked hard and consistently exceeded the expectations that were placed on me to do my job, but the truth is, I was operating within an uneasy truce with those around me. I became disenchanted with the tension that being right seemed to create in others, so I became an entrepreneur. If you ask me why I left Xerox, I know that I could give you any number of reasons why. The real truth is that I left Xerox so I could be right.

For those who want to pay the price for being right by either leaving, or feeling the indignity of being asked to leave, it seems that a common answer is to become an entrepreneur. It's an answer, but it isn't necessarily the right answer. In my case I wasn't courageous, and I wasn't right; I was lucky. If I could jump into the Way-Back-Machine and sit down with a young, starry-eyed Rob Jolles who was hell bent on being right, I'd tell him a few things that he needed to hear.

Not a Blog ~ Not an Article ~ A Blarticle®

- I'd tell him not to confuse the courage to stand up for what you believe in, with the proper time and place to take that stand.
- I'd tell him not to confuse the pride of ownership of an idea or belief, with the importance of being a functioning, supportive team player who can support the ideas of others.
- I'd tell him not to confuse accepting the rejection of an idea I put forth with selling out.
- I'd tell him to stop focusing on what's written on his tombstone, and instead, learn to focus on having the courage to be wrong sometimes.

When you go to a job interview, you want to be seen as someone who is a team player. You want to let them know you can support the ideas of others, and that you understand there is a time and place to be right. This is not taught in business classes, and I cannot find a Way-Back-Machine. All I can do is work within the present and try and spare others the misfortune of confusing being right with being an asset to a company, and a team. Forget about tombstones, and remember that being right can come at a severe cost. If you've paid that price, learn from it and evolve. It's never too late to learn how to be wrong.[1]

---

1. The 750-word… usually rule was broken yet again. I won't do it again!

Recently, I was approached by the MC of a meeting about the proper pronunciation of my name. He was going to be introducing me as the speaker, so he wanted to get it right. I told him exactly how to pronounce it, although I quietly hoped he would get it wrong. I'll tell you why when you read…

The Pursuit of Imperfection

Pushing ourselves to do our best is clearly one of the keys to success. However, don't confuse the noble act of trying our best with the noble act of pushing ourselves to perfection. They may sound similar but they are dramatically different. Doing our best requires a discipline to take no shortcuts in our effort, and perform at our very finest. But perfection is a whole different story, and the pursuit of it can do far more to destroy what we are putting forward than to perfect it.

We can control our effort, but we cannot control our outcome. Remembering this helps us to optimize both.

It's not a crime to purse perfection; it's just a mistake. If even one shred of evidence existed to prove otherwise, I'd be a fan of perfection, but in fact, the pursuit of perfection only works against us. After all, one of the greatest strengths we possess - when we perform at our highest level - is the ability to perform unencumbered by tension. Do you believe, for one second, that focusing on perfection will *decrease* tension?

Perfection happens on rare occasions, but it is not something that the best of the best actively try to achieve. If you ask someone who actually achieves perfection, he or she will almost always tell you that they did not even contemplate perfection while attempting to accomplish it. They knew that the mere thought of it would create tension, and so that moves them further away from it. When a pitcher is pitching late in a ballgame, and in the position to possibly pitch a perfect game, watch how carefully the other players do all they can to *not* focus on the potential feat at hand. Other than pitching performances and bowling, there is almost no sport or occupation that even allows for perfection and yet, instinctively, we seem determined to pursue it.

I say, let's pursue imperfection! Let's give ourselves a pep talk and remind ourselves of this: Our imperfections, and our ability to deal with what happens when we are outside of our comfort zone, is what will truly impress people. Instead of fearing what might go wrong, why not embrace what might go wrong as an opportunity to show others the *real* you?

When things go wrong, we allow those who are judging us to see a more intimate, and unrehearsed, side of us. Typically, these moments cannot be planned for because they often happen organically, but that spontaneous side of ourselves is what many really want to see. When we have to deal with an unforeseen situation, it shows others how we behave under pressure, in the real world. This human side lets others see your true character. Fashion designer and author Lauren Conrad once said:

"Imperfection is relatable."

I once heard a story about Richard Harris that truly illustrates this point. He had played the part of King Arthur in Camelot, countless times over the course of his career. During a performance in his later years, he actually forgot the words to one of his signature songs. Although the orchestra attempted to cover for him, he signaled the orchestra to stop playing the song. For a brief moment, the audience gasped as he walked towards them and said, "I must confess, I have forgotten the words. Perhaps, if it is not too much trouble, you could help me to remember them." There wasn't a dry eye in the building as the audience stood in unison and sang, together, the immortal

"Camelot." I'm quite sure it was an experience that no one in attendance would ever forget. I wish I had been there.

The pursuit of perfection is a noble cause, but the acceptance of imperfection can actually give you a wonderful opportunity to just be you. If you can embrace the imperfections when they make their surprise appearances, you will find that it will bring you closer to those around you. Your smile and easygoing attitude will be on display and will win over everyone there... and they'll love you for it!

W hen you watch a professional basketball game, you'll see a fast-paced sporting event. One reason for this is that the players are forced to shoot the ball within a specific time period. You'll see how we can apply this same technique to the way we communicate when you read...

The Communication Shot Clock

I was a lucky kid for many reasons, and one reason was because I had a dad, Lee Jolles, who taught me many amazing things. One of the best things he taught me was something he didn't realize he was teaching me. You see, like most parents, my dad always wanted to hear about my day. He would pull up a chair, look me in the eye, and lock into whatever words of mine would follow... for about 45 seconds. Then, he would drift away; first mentally, and then physically. As a child, that didn't make me feel great, but his actions taught me an immensely important communication tactic. You see, either consciously, or unconsciously, he was teaching me about the "communication shot clock."

In basketball, there's a shot clock designed to speed up the flow of the game. Football also has a clock moving the game along, and it looks like baseball will follow. These clocks are designed to increase the pace of the game, and to hold our attention.

Let's face it: We are living in a society that demands that we pick up the pace on just about everything we do, particularly on how we communicate. Emails are faster, books are smaller; tweets are limiting the number of characters we can utilize, and blogs, (or Blarticles®,) are crisper. Each form of communication is attempting to achieve the same goal. That goal is to hold the attention of the viewer.

I think my dad would have been thrilled. He wanted his information quickly, and he wanted the most significant parts identified. Perhaps the most important thing was that if he wanted to learn more, he'd ask for it. As a five-year-old, I may have had a tendency to ramble a bit when I communicated, but as an eight year old, I didn't. I learned how to address a question, provide an intriguing response, and finish my response unrushed – all in 45 seconds or less. Rather than provide multiple examples to a given point, I'd provide my best example. Rather than try and guess which part of the story he might like the best, I'd let him decide. Rather than guess how long to speak for, I had my own, unofficial clock. A communication shot clock can be applied to so many scenarios.

- When we sell, and it's our turn to talk, we don't need to ramble on and on about a solution. We need to succinctly tie the needs of the client to the benefits of our solution.
- When we are in an interview, we don't need to ramble on and on about ourselves. We need to succinctly tie the needs of the employer to the strengths that we bring to the table.
- When we write, we don't need to ramble on and on about our topic. We need to succinctly provide value to those who have been gracious enough to read our words.

According to the National Center for Biotechnology Information, the average attention span of a human being has dropped from twelve seconds in the year 2000 to eight seconds in 2013. We now have the dubious distinction of having an attention span that is one second less than that of a goldfish.

Well, I believe we can do better than a goldfish! I think if we choose our words carefully, our communication shot clock can be stretched to 45 seconds. What's more, when we work with a communication shot clock, we eliminate the guesswork of trying to determine what would be most interesting to our listener. Instead, we can present a clear message, and then let the listener decide what he or she may find the most interesting. The response will let us know what area the listener wants to hear more about. My Dad may have been tough on me as a young child, but I am immensely grateful that he taught me the value of communication that is crisp and to the point.

It seems that, far too often, we are placed in high-pressure situations. To succeed, we need to be able to control our emotions and be truly in the moment. What if there was a way to maximize your performance and calm your emotions? I believe there is, and I'll tell exactly what it is when you read...

Playing the Course – Not the Opponent

Let me begin by saying that I am not much of a golfer. I've just never had the time to work on my golfing skills. When business was strong, I had no time to play. When business was not strong, why would I have been out playing golf? But I have played the game, and at times fairly well, and I respect the game.

There is one interesting aspect of golf that used to puzzle me: Why do professional golfers, when they are in competitions, refuse to look at the scoreboard? They can play for four days, meticulously keeping track of every shot they take, and yet they seem totally uninterested in what their fellow competitors are up to. If they do take a peek, it won't be until the final hole or two. This isn't just something you'll find with a quirky player or two. This is something almost all of the great players do.

I played and coached a lot of basketball and I can tell you, I *always* had a good look at the scoreboard. Based on what I was seeing, I made certain adjustments to counteract what my opponent was doing. After all, I needed my team to be playing strategically. It was important for me to keep track of what our opponent was up to.

It seems that the elite golfers go about things in a completely different manner. To be elite, they have to master the physical game of golf at a level that many of us cannot even comprehend. But that's only half of what it takes to be an elite golfer: They also have to master the mental side of the game. They have to quiet their emotions, focus completely, and have complete confidence in every swing they take. Does this sound like a mindset you could benefit from?

Think about the last time you had an important sales call with a potential client, or a critical interview you were prepping for. What mindset did you subscribe to? For most, it's the mindset of a typical competitor: You split your time preparing for what you could and could not control. The "could control" items gave you confidence. These were things like the questions you would ask, the materials you would prepare, and your overall preparation and execution. These types of things gave you confidence because they were 100% within your control.

Here's the thing: You also unwittingly devoted a great deal of time to the "could not" control items. These were things like what your competition might be up to, or your competition's overall preparation or execution. You may have even worried about some of the politics that might be behind the client or the job you were attempting to land. I suppose that, on some level, these were all legitimate worries, but these were worries you had absolutely no control over. So how does worrying about your opponent's performance help your performance? Do you see the genius behind the elite golfer's mindset now?

Control what you can control; *your* game, *your* preparation, *your* execution. Play the course to the best of your ability, and don't be distracted by your opponent. You will be able to quiet your emotions and you'll be able to focus completely on what you are there to do. If you can do that, you will be able to perform at your absolute optimum level. What else can you hope for?

You have zero control over your opponent's performance. If someone better comes along, who is legitimately better suited for the job, there isn't anything you can do. As long as you know you gave your very best, you'll feel okay. If the nephew of the boss gets the job, or the budget wasn't appropriate to begin with, or the company just doesn't like _____ (fill in the blank,) why add this to your worries? These things were never in your control to begin with, so there was no use in spending your energy worrying about it.

By playing the course without obsessing about the opponent, you not only improve your ability to quiet your emotions, focus, and perform with confidence, but you also will have the privilege of doing what you do best: You will be able to confidently show how very special you are.

I am not a fisherman, nor will I ever become one, but it was a fisherman who taught me a valuable lesson about how we judge ourselves. It's a lesson I'd love to share with you when you read…

The Fisherman's Bucket

Fishing fascinates me. My Dad loved to fish. My nephew Matt loves to fish. Quite frankly, I've never really understood what's so interesting about sitting or standing around, for hours at a time, with a pole in your hand… but I learned a valuable lesson from a fisherman.

Some time ago, I was wandering around the banks of the Potomac River and I came across a fisherman. He seemed happy enough, sitting there with his pole in the water. I smiled, and instinctively asked him the only question I knew to ask a fisherman: "Did you catch anything?"

He politely smiled and nodded rather ambivalently. I had no idea what that nod meant and my brain began to swirl with more questions like, "So, *did you* catch anything?!" "How many fish did you catch?" and "How big was the fish you caught?" I wanted to ask these questions because, in a sense, I was trying to judge whether he was successful at what he was doing or not.

Still curious, I tried to sneak a peak into his bucket where I assumed he was keeping the fish he may or may not have caught. Unfortunately, the lid was covering part of the bucket so I shrugged my shoulders and began to leave. He must have sensed that I wasn't satisfied with his response because he called out to me. He told me something I have never forgotten…

"You want to know how many fish I've caught because you think the more fish I catch, the happier I'll be. For a real fisherman, one has nothing to do with the other. I'm out here on a beautiful morning, amongst spectacular nature, along the banks of a magnificent river. I'm having a wonderful day because I love to fish; not because of what's in the bucket. If that's not good enough for you, move the lid and look in the bucket." So, I did.

His response made me think about my triathlon and marathon days. It took a lot of work to get ready for those races, and it was a tremendous challenge to complete them. For some of those races, it took years of training to be able to even participate in them. People who have never run a race would ask me what my time was. People who actually did run in races asked only one question: "Did you finish?"

This concept of defining success by *your* goals, and not the goals of others, translates to much of what we do.

- Sometimes it's pursuing a career that doesn't generate a lot of money, but we find personally fulfilling and satisfying.
- Sometimes it's pursuing a client who may not end up working with us, but for whom we complete a proposal that is on time and to the best of our ability.
- Sometimes it's delivering a presentation to an audience that just isn't very responsive, but we know that we prepared diligently and brought our "A-game" delivery skills.

There are so many scenarios that seem to trap us into judging our success by the outcome rather than our effort. These scenarios seem to focus on what we cannot control, rather than on what we can control. These scenarios often define something we do by how conventional thinking judges our accomplishments, rather than the joy we feel simply doing something we love.

Now, would you still like to know what I saw in that fisherman's bucket? If you do, read this Blarticle® again.

During a recent trip to a driving range, I was reminded of the most fundamental lesson involved in learning any new skill, and one that ultimately decides whether you'll be good, or great, at any task that requires a process. I'll tell you what that lesson is, and how to make that lesson work for you when you read…

Getting Good at Doing Things Badly

Think about the last time you learned a new, and difficult, process. You may not have known it then, but learning that process was the easy part. *Implementing* it, however, was almost always the hard part. It really comes down to one simple question: Do you want to marginally improve, or do you want to pour your heart and soul into succeeding?

I find myself thinking about a crossroads many are faced with when learning the game of golf. Watch amateur golfers warming up or playing, and you'll see exactly what I mean. In a sense, you'll be looking at two types of golfers.

One type of golfer is not very good at what he or she is doing. This person has been hitting the ball improperly for so long that they are actually good at hitting the ball badly! Let's assume there were lessons involved, and perhaps a few of the ideas taught were partially adhered to. There was probably some practice too, but practice is not a lot of fun, so there wasn't much. There was also a nagging voice that said, "Come on, you're thinking about this so much! You're actually worse now than before you took these lessons! Grab a technique or two, learn it your way, and let's get back to getting that ball in the fairway."

There was no other voice that tried to shout back; what had begun as a strict new way of doing things slowly became a distant memory with a stray idea or two done halfway. That particular person will continue to play the game at an amateur level, expecting more, changing little, and baffled by his or her lack of success.

The other type of golfer is very good at what he or she is doing. This success did not come by accident, nor through a series of shortcuts. I can almost guarantee you that there were lessons involved, and more importantly, those lessons were strictly adhered to. There was practice, and a lot of it. There was also a nagging voice that tried to con that golfer away from his or her disciplined approach: "Come on, this is just too hard. You got the ball in the fairway before these lessons, and you played a decent game of golf! Not only that – you had fun!"

But that voice was shouted down by another voice that said something like this: "No, I'm going to master this, and that means I'm going to take a step or two back before I move forward." That golfer went from playing the game in a satisfactory manner, to playing worse for a brief period, and then ultimately being able to play the game at a much higher level than he or she had ever imagined. That type of golfer is able to achieve a high level of success and enjoyment in playing the game.

The moral of this story is this: When you work at doing something incorrectly long enough, you can actually get good at doing it… badly. But make no mistake about it: No matter how much harder you work, your level of improvement will level off at good, and you will *never* be great.

On the other hand, if you work at doing something correctly that is truly challenging, you will almost always get worse before you get better. However, the harder you work, the greater your improvement will be, and the ultimately stronger level of skill you will achieve. You *will* be great!

When you want to perfect those challenging skills, you will probably have to learn a new, well-organized process. There won't be much luck involved; it is will be a matter of hard work and discipline. Be aware, however, of that voice that will tell you to go back to your old way of doing things. After all, you can get good and doing things badly.

Have you ever tried to teach another person how to play chess? I recently tried to teach one of my kids, and I never made it past my introduction to the pawn. That's because, although overlooked by most, the pawn is a fascinating chess piece; it inspired me, and it might just inspire you when you read…

The Perfect Underdog

When was the last time you tried to teach another person how to play chess? It's no easy task. Recently, one of my kids expressed interest so I decided to have a go at it. Clearly, I was feeling ambitious.

I began my lesson with what I felt was the easiest piece on the board; the pawn. For those who don't play chess, a pawn is a chess piece that represents the smallest size and value. A pawn can only move one square forward (or two on the first move), or one square diagonally forward when capturing an opponent's piece. They are pretty expendable and as such, each player begins with eight pawns.

I think the poor pawn has a bit of an image problem. The pawn is perceived as a very weak piece on the board, and the word "pawn" is a fairly unflattering label to attach to another person. Webster's Dictionary defines the word "pawn" as "a person used by others for their own purposes." Ouch.

The Urban Dictionary takes an even tougher stance on the poor pawn. It has 2 definitions: 1. Someone who is used or manipulated to further another person's purposes. 2. A person who is a fool. Clearly no one in his or her right mind would ever want to be called a pawn… or would you?

There's more to the pawn then meets the eye, and as I began to wrap up my explanation of this apparently unfortunate piece, I was reminded of one, last, rather obscure quality of a pawn. The pawn is the only piece on the board that has the ability to do more - much more. The rules state that if a pawn can make it to the other side of the board without being captured, it "promotes." This means that the owner of the pawn can replace it with any other piece desired other than a king. As the queen is the most powerful and versatile piece on the board, that's usually the piece selected most often.

So, let's review. The pawn is the chess piece that is known as the weakest on the chessboard, it poses the least threat, and it is so undervalued that it is actually a personal insult if connected to an actual human being. This same piece also has the ability to become the most powerful piece on the board. What do you think of the pawn now? Personally, I think the pawn makes the perfect underdog. We can learn a lesson or two from this pawn; in order for it to become powerful, two things need to occur:

1. Skill. Maneuvering a pawn completely across the chess board, one space at a time, vulnerable from all positions, and unable to move at all if a piece gets in front of it, takes a *lot* of talent. Like most things in life, it takes a *lot* of hard work to become great at the game of chess.
2. Luck. All the skill in the world still won't ensure the pawn's success. There is always an element of luck involved. But as Thomas Jefferson famously said, "I'm a greater believer in luck, and I find the harder I work, the more I have of it."

Aren't those a couple of tactics that would affect your personal success as well? With hard work that transfers to actual skill… and a little bit of luck, that underestimated underdog pawn can be transported from being the weakest piece on the board to the strongest piece on the board. The next time you feel undervalued, let the pawn inspire you to work hard, take control of your own luck, and show others you have the ability to accomplish great things!

Final Thoughts

You made it! You've reached the final pages of this personally curated collection. I hope you've found insights that resonate, lessons that inspire, and strategies that empower you in journey in persuasion, performance, and personal growth. These Blarticles® have been more than just words on a page for me—they've been a long journey of discovery, shared with you in the hope that they spark new ideas and perspectives in your own journey.

Whether you apply these lessons in business, leadership, or personal challenges, remember that growth is a continuous process. Keep learning, keep refining, and most importantly, keep taking action.

Thank you for allowing me to share these stories and insights with you. The journey doesn't end here—so go forth, apply what you've learned, and make your own mark on the world. Feel free to write some of your own Blarticles®, and when you do, put its registered trademark symbol (®) after it, and make sure it is:

a concise, impactful piece of writing that delivers meaningful insights in a way that is both engaging and educational – in 750 words or less… usually. (I won't tell if you don't.)

With gratitude and best wishes,

PS - If you've ever wanted to hear what it sounds like when I read a Blarticle®, follow my Pocket Sized Pep Talks podcast and you'll hear a new one every Wednesday.

Also by Rob Jolles

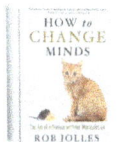  

How to Change Minds

Customer Centered Selling

Why People Don't Believe You

How to Run Seminars & Workshops

The Way of the Road Warrior

About Jolles Associates, Inc.

For more information regarding keynotes, and workshops available:

***Visit:* www.jolles.com**

Email: training@jolles.com or *Call:* (703) 759-7767

To sign up for the Blarticle® visit www.jolles.com/blarticle

To follow Rob's "Pocket Sized Pep Talks" Podcasts:

https://podcasts.apple.com/us/podcast/pocket-sized-pep-talks/id1497772972

Tune in and get inspired!

Connect on LinkedIn https://www.linkedin.com/in/rob-jolles and follow his biweekly newsletter:

"When Every Word Matters." www.linkedin.com/in/rob-jolles-8a459b12

- Follow Rob's YouTube channel and you'll have access to a wealth of podcasts and more, designed to help you to communicate with impact.

YouTube Channel: https://www.youtube.com/user/robjolles